THE PHOTOGRAPHS OF ARᴄʜɪᴇ ᴄʜɪꜱHOLM

Michael Cope was born in London in 1949 and trained as a geologist to pursue a career in the international petroleum industry. He first became interested in the Outer Hebrides when studying the South Harris geological complex as an undergraduate. Several decades later he renewed his interest in the islands through his wife's family history and Archie Chisholm's photographs. Michael now lives in Dorking, Surrey and is currently researching the history of post offices in the Outer Isles.

THE PHOTOGRAPHS OF ARCHIE CHISHOLM

Life and Landscapes in the Outer Hebrides 1881–1913

MICHAEL COPE

THIRSTY BOOKS
EDINBURGH

Published in 2018 by Thirsty Books, Edinburgh
thirstybooks.com

ISBN: 978-0-9932828-5-0

Printed and bound by Bell & Bain Ltd, Glasgow

Typeset by Main Point Books, Edinburgh
mainpointbooks.co.uk

Dedicated to the memory of
Alastair Francis Chisholm
1941–2010

Archibald Alexander ('Archie') Chisholm 1859–1933

Contents

Preface

A unique and remarkable archive of photographs was produced by Archibald Alexander ('Archie') Chisholm while he was Procurator Fiscal in Lochmaddy, North Uist (then part of insular Inverness-shire), from 1881 to 1913. Archie was a keen observer of people and places and chronicler of events throughout the islands and in all nearly three hundred separate images have been attributed as taken through the lens of his camera. Grouping these images together by theme rather than just place has allowed for a clear narrative of late Victorian/early Edwardian Hebridean life to emerge, one that has not previously been presented in this way. Comparing these historical images with present day photographs of the same scenes serves to illustrate the changes, or sometimes lack of them, across the islands in the intervening hundred or so years.

Archie Chisholm was my wife's grandfather and my involvement with this project started about ten years ago when I began to assist my brother-in-law Alastair Chisholm, Archie's grandson, in researching a collection of family photographs from the 1890s and 1900s. It soon became apparent that these photographs were part of a more extensive and historically important archive which captured many aspects of Outer Hebridean life and landscapes during those decades. The photographs were taken in the years 1892 to 1906 when Archie was living and working in Lochmaddy. These were interesting and changing times in the Hebrides – land agitation and the eventual passing of the Crofters' Act, new steamship communications, development of sporting estates and tourist hotels, expansion of the fishing industry, a major period of church construction and the coming of the first motor transports. I have tried to cover these topics with appropriate photographs, but ultimately I have been limited to the extent of Archie's archive – it is hoped there is enough variety to do justice to all these subjects.

Any book of this kind relies on the knowledge and contributions of others. The original concept was the brainchild of Alastair Chisholm, who sadly died in 2010, and I have benefited greatly from his early template of the project and use of his notes and files to produce what is presented here. I hope that it would meet with Alastair's approval were he able to see the final outcome. Archie's other grandchildren, Peter Chisholm, Colin Chisholm and Elizabeth Cope and Alastair's wife Catherine Third have also given a great deal of support to the project at different times. Annie Cope, Archie's great-granddaughter, provided her valuable professional assistance in formatting the picture illustrations.

I am very grateful to Norman MacLeod of Taigh Chearsabhagh, Lochmaddy, North Uist and Sue Wilson and Hector MacAuley of the North Uist Historical Society who kindly read and commented on an early draft of the manuscript; Sue and Hector's advice on the use of Gaelic in the text was particularly useful. Professor James Hunter of the University of the Highlands and Islands kindly reviewed the section on crofting communities which was based on his published studies of the topic. Thanks are due to the following who have helped with materials, logistics, enquiries and invaluable local knowledge: Hamish Johnson of Floddabay, Harris; Norman Johnson of Lochmaddy, North Uist; Bill Lawson of Northton, Harris; James Matheson of Claddach Kirkibost, North Uist; George MacDonald of Stornoway, Lewis, formerly factor of the North Uist Estate; John MacDonald of Lochmaddy, North Uist; Alasdair MacEachen of South Uist; Roderick MacLeod of Furnace, Argyll; John Maclennan of Stornoway, Lewis; Margaret Paterson of Berneray; Tony Scherr of Borve, Harris; and all those islanders who have pointed me in the right direction on my travels – as Alastair was always reminding me, 'never underestimate the importance of local knowledge, even a hundred years after the event'.

In connection with the studies of the picture postcards, the following have assisted in generously providing scans of their own collections to supplement those in the family's possession: Norman Hudson, Sandra Charnley, Marjorie Gardner and Mike Ellis. Additionally, Norman Hudson kindly reviewed the section concerning postal history and contributed his personal knowledge of the subject. Roger Miket at Maclean Press granted permission to reproduce figures from Bob Charnley's original books featuring Archie's postcards. Edwina Fassom is thanked for drafting the location maps in Appendix 1.

Grateful acknowledgements are due to the National Museums of Scotland (NMS) and the National Library of Scotland (NLS) for permissions to reproduce images from their Scottish Life Archive and map collections respectively. Other sources are acknowledged in the text as appropriate.

Finally, my grateful thanks are due to Sean Bradley at Thirsty Books and Jennie Renton at Main Point Books for turning Alastair's and my ideas, notes and picture files into the book that the reader is now holding and hopefully will enjoy reading.

Michael Cope, Dorking, Surrey, October 2018

Fig. 1.1: Alastair Chisholm at the ruins of Rhu-na-gall, Lochmaddy, in 2004. This was the house first rented by Archie Chisholm on his appointment as Procurator Fiscal in Lochmaddy in 1881 [Photograph: Catherine Third].

Chapter 1

THE PROJECT

For some years Alastair Chisholm, Archibald Alexander ('Archie') Chisholm's grandson, and my brother-in-law, had been researching a collection of old family photographs known to have been taken while his grandfather was the Procurator Fiscal in Lochmaddy during the years 1881–1913. The research led Alastair to start to establish the locations of the photographs and capture present day images of the same views, literally following in his grandfather's footsteps from Barra to Harris. I joined him to assist in the fieldwork in Harris in 2007. Sadly Alastair died in 2010, but using his files, notes and photographs I continued to undertake the research which has ultimately led to this publication.

Finding some of the locations has not been easy and we suspect that is in part because Archie used a pony to get his equipment to some of the more remote spots. We dispensed with using a pony as our digital cameras fitted conveniently into a rucksack! Also, with the new roads and causeways constructed throughout the islands in the 1960s and 1970s, some of the aspects for the original photographs are no longer available, but we have done our best.

Use of the Photographic Archive

As the project expanded it became apparent that, in addition to the photographic prints in possession of the Chisholm family, there were many more images to be found in the Scottish Life Archive of the NMS, Edinburgh, and there existed a series of picture postcards produced by Archie as a commercial venture. Subsequent researches also unearthed a set of lantern slides and yet more prints in the hands of other private collectors.

To date, over 280 separate images have been found spread equally across the photographic prints and the picture postcards.

Appendix 1 provides a comprehensive listing of all the images, the dates they were taken where available, and their locations with National Grid References where these can be determined. Each image has been assigned a unique identifying number and this is quoted in the figure captions for ease of reference to the listing. Many of the photographs have been included in the Scottish Life Archive of the NMS and their catalogue numbers are also included in the listing.

A Note on the Use of Gaelic

It is apparent in the handwritten annotations on his photographs and in the captions on his picture postcards that Archie used a mix of English and Gaelic descriptions of both places and subjects. Most were in English, but it is also clear that when he employed Gaelic he was not entirely precise in his use of the language. In addition he was not consistent in the transliteration of place names from Gaelic into English. This confusion is compounded by the fact that different editions of maps over the last century have also offered different spellings of place names. Faced with this differential usage, the following conventions have been adopted:

1. The descriptions of photographs and captions of picture postcards are given in the form as originally recorded in either English or Gaelic (see Appendix 1 for a full listing).

2. Where figure captions quote English or Gaelic descriptions derived from the photographs or picture postcards translations are only given from either language where deemed necessary for clarification.

3. Gaelic terms introduced in the text are shown in italics with an English translation provided where necessary.

4. As most of the books and reference documents of the day used in this research listed place names in English then this convention is followed in the text.

5. Gaelic translations and their alternatives for English place names used in the text are provided in a glossary included as Appendix 2. The definitive spellings of Gaelic place names are taken from the latest editions of 1:25,000 Ordnance Survey Maps.

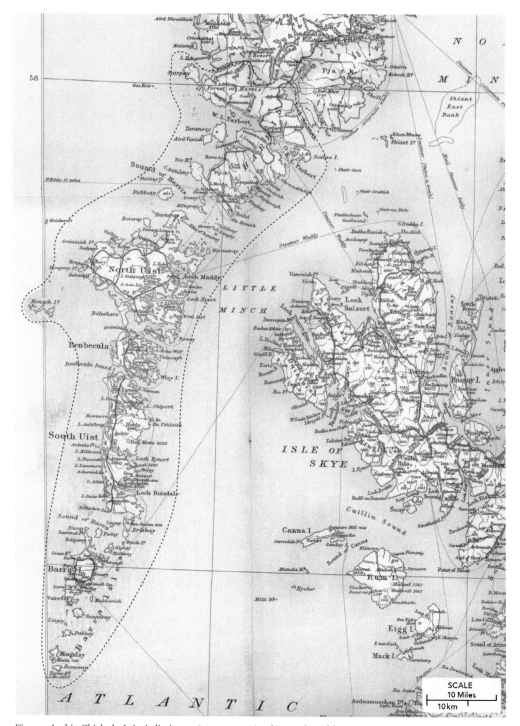

Fig. 2.1: Archie Chisholm's jurisdiction as Procurator Fiscal in Lochmaddy, comprising the Inverness-shire part of the 'Long Island' (red dashed line). [Illustration taken from Bartholomew's *Tourist Map of Scotland Showing the New County Boundaries*, published in 1892; reproduced by permission of the NLS].

Chapter 2

ARCHIE CHISHOLM, FISCAL IN LOCHMADDY

Archibald Alexander ('Archie') Chisholm was born at Achnacloich, Kiltarlity, Inverness-shire on 28th January 1859, the eldest surviving son of Aeneas Chisholm and his second wife, Flora MacDonald. On leaving school he followed a legal career, apparently without any university training, and by 1878 had by an 'apprenticeship' become Sheriff-Clerk Depute to Sir Henry C. MacAndrew in Inverness. At that time Archie is listed among members of the Gaelic Society of Inverness as living at Phopachy, Inverness; he remained a member of the society until at least 1894. At the 1881 census Archie was living with his uncle Theodore at Innes Street, Inverness and was later that year appointed Procurator Fiscal at Lochmaddy, a position he occupied for 32 years, his area of jurisdiction covering the Inverness-shire part of the 'Long Island' (Fig. 2.1). While at Lochmaddy, he also acted as a member of the North Uist School Board and as clerk to the School Board of South Uist.

At his leaving presentation in 1913, as reported in the *Oban Times*, he was presented with 'a handsome silver epergne and a purse of sovereigns', and his wife was 'the recipient of a lovely pearl and diamond pendant'. In his presentation address his erstwhile colleague Thomas Wilson remarked on 'Mr Chisholm's fitness for the high office that had been conferred on him':

> During 32 years of his residence in the district, Mr Chisholm had done more perhaps than anyone towards raising the moral and material condition of the people in the Long Island: to his efforts in a great measure they owed the excellent postal, telegraph and steamer communications they now enjoyed.

Recalling Archie's direct professional duties, Wilson went on to observe that:

> As Procurator Fiscal, he had always acted with the utmost impartiality, administering equal justice to rich and poor and refusing to be coerced by any sort of influence from close adherence to the path of duty. They all knew with what consummate skill he managed affairs at the time of the land agitation, and the people of the Long Island would remember that it was due to his judicious handling of a very delicate situation that military and marines were not sent among them in these troubled times.

In his reply, Archie, recalling his time in office, said:

> All I can claim is that I have tried to do fairly to all classes, without fear or favour, affection or ill-will. Through it all I have been sustained by what is, perhaps, the cleanest, fairest, and best Government department in Scotland – the department of the Crown Office and the Lord Advocate. There, no matter what political party ruled, any man whose rights or liberties were in question received even-handed justice.

And, referring to the land agitation issue, he commented:

> As a matter of fact both parties, from different points of view, were always glad to get a solution to the troubles that arose. We never required the military or marines here although at one time there was a proposal made that they should be stationed from Barra Head to the March of Lewis [the Inverness-shire part of the Long Island]. The Home Secretary of the day, however, recognised that any such action would be an uncalled for offence to a peaceable people.

This belief in and pursuit of an even-handed approach to justice was perhaps at the root of the enmity between him and Sir John Campbell-Orde, the owner of the North Uist Estate, which ultimately led to Archie being left without any permanent residence in Lochmaddy in 1891. Indeed, Sir John did not have much time for the legal protections given to his tenants under the 1886 Crofters' Act and continued in acts of harassment in spite of the law.

As well as being Procurator Fiscal, Archie also had a solicitor's practice in Lochmaddy, Chisholm & Co, at which Thomas Wilson worked as a solicitor. The firm had refused to act for Sir John in connection with eviction disputes with his tenants. Moreover Wilson was happy to act for the tenants seeking to avoid eviction, believing that Sir John was engaged in harassment. Archie also was initially happy to act for the tenants, but then later agreed not to on advice of the Sheriff, seeing a conflict with his role as Procurator Fiscal. This apparent conflict within the firm probably led to the dissolution of the Chisholm & Co partnership. Sir John's anger with Wilson eventually boiled over leading to him being forbidden in 1889 to take lodgings at any house on the Estate; he had to resort to living on a boat in Lochmaddy harbour. These issues smouldered away between Sir John and it seems the entire legal profession so that by 1891 when the Procurator Fiscal's lease of a house from the Estate came up for renewal another bitter wrangle ensued.

Archie's first residence in Lochmaddy was *Rhuir* cottage (now known to have actually been *Rhu-na-gall*, subsequently demolished in 2007; Fig. 2.2) on which he took a ten-year lease from the Estate of Sir John Campbell-Orde. The lease ran from Martinmas (11th November) 1881 to Martinmas 1891 with an annual rent of £30. Although wishing to renew the lease, he had been in dispute with Sir John since 1889 over 'arrears' for cottages built in Lochmaddy for his clerks. Archie was also disputing the non-reimbursement of a sum of £150 which he had paid for essential repairs to the

Fig. 2.2: *Rhu-na-gall* in 2004. This was the house referred to in Archie's 1881–1891 lease as *Rhuiar* (in fact a quite separate cottage built much later in 1923); the house was demolished in 2007 [Photograph: Alastair Chisholm].

property. As a result, Sir John issued Archie with a notice to quit on 6th October 1891 and refused to let him any other property in North Uist or to even let him stay at the hotel in Lochmaddy. On 14th November 1891 correspondence from Archie to Sir John indicates that he was:

> greatly vexed and injured by having to obey your formal notices to remove and that I cannot get another house here. A local gentleman has, however, extended hospitality to me which enables me to stay at Lochmaddy for the present.

It is likely that the gentleman referred to was James M. Fraser, the Agent for the Caledonian Banking Company, and that the place where he stayed was The Bank House in Lochmaddy (Fig. 2.3). It seems this became Archie's lodgings for the next seven years as the dispute with Sir John could not be resolved and Archie was prohibited to rent or build a house anywhere on the Campbell-Orde estate. Archie's correspondence shows that after his eviction he considered that Sir John was purposely harassing an officer of the Crown; writing on 22nd March 1892 he states:

> I was compelled to sell off my effects at a heavy loss. Every ingenuity has been used to harass me by withholding monies not questioned to be due to me, and by now making for articles I was induced not to sell (as they were beneficial to the holding), on the day of my sale upon the agreement that I would get paid for them – ridiculously low offers, in consequence of which I have had to place the latter in the hands of an agent.

Public auctions of personal effects following deaths, evictions or bankruptcies were common in the 1890s. Archie caught on camera an auction of household effects at the house of the late Mr MacAlpine, a Free Church Minister, in Clachan a' Luib, North Uist in April 1897 (Figs. 2.4 & 2.5). Perhaps the scene appealed to him as a way to document his own experiences a few years earlier.

On 5th July 1892 Archie married Helen Annie McHardy at St Margaret's Church, Kinning Park, Glasgow; Helen Annie was

Fig. 2.3A (below left): The Bank House in Lochmaddy originally belonging to the Caledonian Banking Company; this postcard was probably produced after 1907 as it is captioned 'Bank of Scotland', after the amalgamation of the two companies [*Cairt Phostail* series postcard: 2157].
Fig. 2.3B (below): The Bank House as it appears today. It offers bed and breakfast accommodation so it is again taking lodgers more than one hundred years after Archie's residence [Photograph: Alastair Chisholm].

Fig. 2.4: Public auction at Minister's house in Clachan na Luib, North Uist [Original Archie Chisholm photograph: 1188; image © NMS].

Fig. 2.5: Public auction at Minister's house in Clachan na Luib, North Uist [Original Archie Chisholm photograph: 1189; image © NMS].

the youngest daughter of Alexander McHardy, Chief Constable of Inverness-shire, and his wife Helen Monica (née Grant). Having been forced to sell his household effects at the end of 1891, it seems unlikely that Helen moved to North Uist with Archie at this time, but rather that she stayed in Inverness with her parents in Fairfield Road. Certainly Helen was in Inverness for the birth of her first four children: Flora (b. 1893), Alexander (Alastair, b. 1894), Helen (b. 1896) and Aeneas (b. 1897); sadly Aenas died in infancy in 1898.

The dispute with Sir John escalated over several years while Archie was living at The Bank House. Sir John also refused Archie's request for a feu (a perpetual lease) so that he could build a house to allow the Procurator Fiscal to live independently of any undue influence, this being highlighted in his letter to Sir John on 1st December 1891:

> I must protest against his being judge and ruler of my position past or future. His refusal of a feu or other dwelling-place I take unmistakably to show his real desire is to hold me in a position subject to his favour or fear.

Making little progress with an exchange of letters, Archie eventually arranged for the entire bitter correspondence between them to be published in the *Scottish Highlander* newspaper in February and March 1894;[1] the same correspondence was also appended to Thomas Wilson's evidence to The Royal Commission (Highlands and Islands) given in 1892 and published in 1895.[2]

By 1896 the matter had found its way to Parliament with a question from J. G. Weir the MP for Ross & Cromarty asking the Lord Advocate:[3]

> I beg to ask the Lord Advocate if he is now in a position to state whether the landlord of the Island of North Uist, Inverness-shire, has yet agreed to allow the sheriff substitute and procurator fiscal

at Lochmaddy residence there; and, if not whether arrangements will be made to enable these officials to secure residence in the island?

The Lord Advocate (Graham Murray) replied:

I am glad to be able to inform the Hon. Member, so far as the sheriff substitute is concerned, that lease is now under adjustment; but I am unable to say the same as regards the procurator fiscal. It is to be hoped that the proprietor and the procurator fiscal may eventually arrange the matter in a friendly way, but no power exists to compel proprietors to grant feus or leases to public officials.

Matters appear to have resolved themselves, however, after Sir John's death in 1897 and Archie eventually found a house to rent from the Campbell-Orde estate in Lochmaddy. He leased Ostrom House (Fig. 2.6) to accommodate his wife and family at a rent of £40 per annum from Whitsunday (29th May) 1898 and, additionally from Whitsunday 1899, The Park at a rent of £3 per annum. While at Ostrom three more children were born in the Chisholm family: Mairi (b.1900), Margaret (b. 1903) and Archibald (b.1904).

It was while at Ostrom that Archie took most of his known photographs and produced his *Cairt Phostail* series of picture postcards (see Chapter 3). We have an abundant archive of photographs with dates in the range 1892 to 1904, but, oddly, few photographs dated after this period are known. What we know from Michael Gardner's book *The History of Finsbay Lodge, Harris,*[4] is that sometime after 1903 Archie became a shareholder in the Hebridean Sporting Association – perhaps this became his new passion. Archie rented the various properties in Lochmaddy until Whitsunday 1913, when he returned to Inverness on appointment as Sheriff-Clerk of the County of Inverness.

When back in Inverness Archie pursued several interests

Fig. 2.6A: Ostrom House as it appeared c.1900 in a picture postcard, probably produced by Archie for use by the Chisholm family [3205].

Fig. 2.6B: Ostrom House as it appears today; latterly used as a youth hostel, it is now unoccupied [Photograph: Alastair Chisholm].

outside of practising law, including being the first President of the Inverness Rotary Club and sometime President of the Inverness Scientific Society and Field Club. Through this society he continued his interests in the life and history of the Highlands and Islands contributing several papers to their meetings; unfortunately, he published little of his learning and researches.

Archie died on 22nd February 1933 while living at Ardlarich,

Culduthel Road in Inverness, aged 74. His obituary in the *Inverness Courier* two days later noted that:

> Alike as Procurator Fiscal in Lochmaddy and Sheriff-Clerk in Inverness Mr Chisholm was held in universal esteem, and he conducted the affairs of both these offices with sound judgement and meticulous care.

Chapter 3

THE PHOTOGRAPHS AND PICTURE POSTCARDS

The Photographs

Archie was a late Victorian-Edwardian middle class gentleman. He had varied interests outside his professional life, including archaeology, natural history, field sports – especially fishing – and, importantly for this publication, photography. His involvement with the Hebridean Sporting Association has been very well documented by Michael Gardner in his book *The History of Finsbay Lodge, Harris.*[4] Bob Charnley has also described the connection between Archie's photographic pursuits and the production of a series of picture postcards of the Outer Hebrides in *The Western Isles a Postcard Tour, Volumes 1 & 2.*[5, 6] It is not the intention here to cover the same ground as these previous works more than is necessary, but to concentrate on the photographic images themselves and what they can reveal of the life and landscapes of the Outer Isles during Archie's time in Lochmaddy.

Over 280 photographic images are attributed to Archie Chisholm. These include: 141 known picture postcards from the *Cairt Phostail* series (see Charnley); 7 other personal postcards; 100 images in the Scottish Life Archive of the NMS; 33 other prints in the possession of the Chisholm family or donated by individuals as a result of our research; and 4 illustrations contributed as plates to W. C. Mackenzie's *History of the Outer Hebrides.*[7] Of these images approximately two thirds are considered properly locatable.

Provenance and Attribution of the Photographs

In 2006 Alastair Chisholm recognised that several collections in the Scottish Life Archive (SLA) of the NMS comprised photographs that could be the work of Archie Chisholm. These included original photographic prints drawn from the Archive's Cathcart Collection and Moran Donation and picture postcards from the Archive binder files. As a result of his research Alastair later donated copies of several of Archie's photographs from his personal collection to supplement those in the Cathcart Collection.

The Cathcart Collection takes its name from Mrs Margaret Cathcart who, in 1964, presented the SLA with a group of photographic prints featuring the people and landscape of the Outer Hebrides. Unfortunately, apart from the fact that she had acquired them some years earlier at a jumble sale in Inverness, Mrs Cathcart knew nothing of their origin. The Moran Donation of photographic prints and postcards was presented to the SLA, also in 1964, by Helen Moran. Helen was Archie's niece which indicates how these items came into her possession. Formal attribution of the various collections to Archie is based on several criteria:

1. The Cathcart prints all appear to feature people and places in the Outer Hebrides and to be dateable to the years shortly before and shortly after 1900, the time Archie was in Lochmaddy.
2. The prints are generally similar in both style and subject-matter to Hebridean photographs that can be securely attributed to plates in W. C. Mackenzie's *History of the Outer Hebrides*,[7] and prints in the family's possession.
3. The specific locations of around 50 prints can be identified. Of these, about half feature the area around Lochmaddy, and the rest the area between Barra and Harris, (i.e. the boundaries of Archie's jurisdiction as Procurator Fiscal).

4. The subject matter spans all four seasons of the year, suggesting that their photographer was resident in the islands.
5. The possibility of there having been more than one photographer who fits this description seems unlikely. Other photographers of this date in the Hebrides appear to have been occasional mainland-based visitors who restricted their activities to the more accessible parts of the islands.
6. Given that the Cathcart prints were acquired as a single lot at a jumble sale in Inverness, it seems likely that these had been in the possession of someone living locally. Archie lived in Inverness on his return to the mainland in 1913 until his death in 1933. Additionally, the Moran prints were supplied by a family relative.
7. The inscriptions on the prints indicate that their author travelled widely, was familiar with the people and places of the islands, and probably a Gaelic speaker. Critically, the inscriptions were actually in Archie's handwriting and a number of the prints either had as their subjects, or included, members of his family.

An additional collection of prints became known to me through Tony Scherr of Borve Lodge, Harris. This comprised a number of original prints reported by Emily MacDonald of Stornoway, in a letter of 12th May 1976 to Reverend Bovey, also of Stornoway, to have been found in a house in Inverness. The prints of Harris were distributed by her to the Harris Hotel, the Rodel Hotel and the remaining nine to Reverend Bovey; the latter then came into the possession of Tony Scherr. Her letter also mentions that some of the prints were sent to Dr MacLeod in North Uist (probably the late Dr Alex MacLeod who died in 1979), but we have no subsequent trace of these.

Another part of the photographic archive is a set of 16 lantern slides in the possession of Mrs Margaret Paterson of Geodhu,

Backhill, Berneray. In 2004 Mrs Paterson told Alastair Chisholm that the slides belonged to her husband, Finlay Paterson, who had inherited them, along with a paraffin-driven projector, a 'magic lantern', from his grandfather, also named Finlay Paterson. The younger Finlay was a ferryman in Berneray, and also the local registrar. Each image, about 6 x 7.5 cm, was contained within two glass plates about 7.5 cm square.

Prints with the same images as the lantern slide set have come to light from various sources including Norman Johnson of Lochmaddy and Reverend Roderick MacLeod of Furnace, Argyll. Both sets of prints are stated to have been produced from original glass plates found in 1970 when cleared from the attic of The Bank House in Lochmaddy; the whereabouts of the plates today is unknown. Whatever their provenance these photographic images, and therefore the lantern slides, are determined to be stylistically similar to the rest of Archie's work and so attributed to him; their association with The Bank House is another reason for their attribution.

These slides and prints include several of the contentious 'eviction' scenes. Controversy surrounds these images – the question is whether the events depicted are the result of tenants being evicted from the land or simply in the process of being rehoused. The issue is discussed further in Chapter 6.

Subjects and Themes

Archie's earliest known photograph is dated April 1892, framed and annotated in his own handwriting, taken of the Smithy at Lochmaddy (Fig. 3.1); the building has long since been demolished.

There is another early photograph known, dated 1892, without month, taken of the steamer and railway terminal at Stromeferry (Fig. 3.2). This is where the steamer service departed for Portree, Tarbert and Lochmaddy before the more established routes

The Smithy, Lochmaddy.
apl. 1892 - J.S.

Fig. 3.1: The Smithy at Lochmaddy, taken in April 1892 [Original Archie Chisholm photograph: 1171; image © NMS].

Fig. 3.2: Stromeferry railway and ferry terminus in 1892, one of Archie's earliest photographs. This view cannot be seen today as the pier has been dismantled [Original Archie Chisholm photograph: 1938; image ©NMS].

Fig. 3.3A (right): Lochmaddy panorama from the Pier Road, probably taken in 1902, the New Courthouse on the left and Ostrom House on the right [Original Archie Chisholm photograph: 1113; image © NMS].

Fig. 3.3B (above): The same Lochmaddy panorama, taken over one hundred years later. The Sheriff Court still sits in the same building. Ostrom House was recently used as a youth hostel, but is now unoccupied [Photograph: Alastair Chisholm].

taken today. Given the year, this might document the start of his journey to life in Lochmadddy as a newly married man, albeit without a permanent home.

Many of Archie's photographs are what might be described as topographical with the themes of landscapes, crofting settlements, villages and public buildings. One photograph illustrated here is particularly noteworthy. It is a panorama of Lochmaddy taken in 1902 showing two buildings important in his life – the New Courthouse and Ostrom House, places where he worked and lived respectively (Fig. 3.3). Archie photographed a number of other Lochmaddy panoramas and several of these are shown in Chapter 9.

Archie also showed a keen eye for portraiture, especially of the crofting and labouring communities and their homes and occupations. A few examples are shown in Figs. 3.4–3.6.

What or who sparked Archie's interest in photography? It is interesting to speculate that he developed his interest through his friendship with Erskine Beveridge, the renowned archaeologist,

Fig. 3.4: Group of labourers at Castlebay, Barra, taken in 1897 [Original Archie Chisholm photograph: 1614; image © NMS].

Fig. 3.5: Crofters – mother, son and lamb! Unlocated and undated [Original Archie Chisholm photograph: 1926; image © NMS].

Fig. 3.6: Pier Master at Lochmaddy Fair, North Uist, taken in 1903 [Original Archie Chisholm photograph: 1145; image © NMS].

Fig. 3.7: A photographer photographed at Lochmaddy cattle fair [Original Archie Chisholm photograph: 1144; image © NMS].

antiquarian and photographer. Beveridge built a house in 1902–1905 on Vallay Island in North Uist at the time Archie was resident in Lochmaddy and in the preface to his book *North Uist: Its Archaeology and Topography*[8] he acknowledges Archie as 'among friends who have been most helpful'. Certainly there is overlap between some of Archie's photographs and the illustrations in Beveridge's book, to the extent that one can envision two photographers side by side taking a similar, but not the same

"Only a drachm!" (Copyright.)

photograph. This speculation perhaps has some substance. One of Archie's photographs taken at a Lochmaddy cattle fair captures a photographer photographing the scene – his back is towards the camera (Fig. 3.7). Could this have been Archie taking a picture of Erskine Beveridge? It looks as if the person taking the photograph has a beard and moustache. Study the photograph and reach your own conclusion...

Fig.3.8A: 'Only a drachm!' an example of the *Cart Phostail* series with the characteristic '(Copyright)' designation attributable to Archie Chisholm. [2902].

The Picture Postcards

While he would probably have been content to be referred to as an 'amateur', the use of the term is somewhat at odds with the fact that, at some time around the early 1900s, Archie had arranged for more than 140 of his 'Hebridean studies' to be professionally printed for sale as postcards (Fig. 3.8). One of the distinguishing features of these cards is that in place of the normal heading 'Post Card' on their

Fig. 3.8B: Address side of the 'Only a drachm!', *Cart Phostail*, showing that this particular example was printed in Germany. The vertical inscription reads '*Ceud-sreath d'n Eilean-Fhad*', ('First Edition of the Long Island').

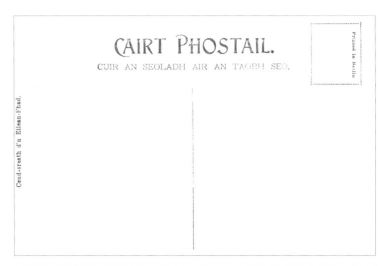

Fig. 3.9: Publicity for printing of pictorial postcards. This example printed on the back of one of Archie's views of Lochmaddy. [Reproduced from: B. Charnley *The Western Isles A Postcard Tour, Vol. 1*].

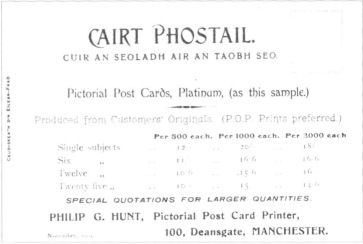

reverse side, they carry the Gaelic equivalent, '*Cairt Phostail*'. The other is that, although the picture-faces of the cards are clearly marked 'Copyright', there is nothing to identify Archie as their photographer. Assuming this omission to have been deliberate, a possible explanation is that, as a public official, Archie may have thought it inappropriate to advertise his involvement in a commercial venture, albeit of a relatively modest nature.

Fig. 3.10: Souvenir picture postcard from the Scottish Home Industries Association Manchester Exhibition in 1903 using one of Archie's photographs and showing a manuscript correction in his handwriting [3622; image © NMS].

Whatever the case, and publicly at least, he was to remain unidentified until some of his cards came to the attention of collector and author Bob Charnley. In the introduction to *The Western Isles: A Postcard Tour*, published in 1992,[5] Charnley describes how his acquisition of a number of cards in what he calls the *Cairt Phostail* series, prompted the research that eventually enabled their attribution to Archie Chisholm.

It is not known who produced all the cards for Archie. Bob Charnley illustrates one postcard with its address side used as publicity for Philip G. Hunt, Pictorial Post Card Printer, 100 Deansgate, Manchester, dated November 1904 (Fig. 3.9).

We also know that several of Archie's images were used on souvenir postcards for the Scottish Home Industries Association Manchester Exhibition in October 1903, so perhaps this is the link with the Manchester printer and helps to provide a framework for the start of Archie's commercial venture as some time in 1903–1904. There are firm links of at least two of these postcards to Archie. Firstly, there is a manuscript correction in his handwriting on a card showing fishermen's huts in Castlebay (Fig. 3.10). Secondly his photograph of boys fishing in Uist (see Fig. 12.9) is also used in the series.

In addition several other postcards in this series are known to me from the collection of Norman Hudson of Chester. Stylistically the images are all quite similar and it is possible that more of the pictures in this series may be attributed to Archie. Perhaps this was the spur for him to go on and produce his own *Cairt Phostail* series.

There are also other *Cairt Phostail* cards that have the inscription 'Printed in Berlin' on their address sides (see Fig. 3.8B), indicating a quite different origin. From their usage patterns it is probable that the cards printed in Germany were produced after 1907. Other differences in the colour and typeface for the '*Cairt Phostail*' inscription suggest that at least six different printings of the cards were undertaken. All the cards, however, bear the Gaelic inscription '*Ceud-sreath d'n Eilean-Fhad*', translated as 'First Edition of the Long Island'. So, one edition or six, where and when printed and by whom remain topics for further research by interested postcard collectors.

Chapter 4

Landscapes

The Underlying Geology

In geological terms the landscape of the Outer Isles is both
very old and very young – ancient bedrock fashioned by recent
ice. Most of the rock outcrops seen throughout the islands are
composed of Lewisian gneiss – typically grey banded and folded
rocks, the result of intense heat and pressure deep in the Earth's
crust, subsequently exposed by eons of uplift and erosion.
These are amongst the oldest rocks on the planet being dated
as up to 2.7 billion years old, about two thirds of the age of the
Earth. The Lewisian terrain produces a generally featureless
landscape over much of the islands. The more mountainous
tracts along the eastern spine of the Uists and in North Harris
are developed where the rocks are more varied, but similarly
of great age.

Lacking in the Outer Hebrides are the much younger volcanic
rocks of the Inner Hebrides related to the development of the
Atlantic Ocean. These date from about 50–60 million years
ago and give rise to flat lava flows, spectacular basalt cliffs and
columns and dark jagged peaks like the Cuillins. As a result the
landscape of the outer islands is softer and generally not so
enclosing. Geologically speaking, the Outer Isles represent a
long-lived continental remnant unaffected by cataclysmic earth
movements happening around it – perhaps a metaphor for life
on the islands!

Also lacking is any significant mineralisation of the rocks,
such as seen in, say, Cornwall or the Lake District, which gave
rise to mining through the 18th and 19th centuries and generated

Fig. 4.1: View of Namh Ardh taken from above Direcleit showing typical landscape of Harris with the ice-fashioned rounded hills of the Forest of Harris in the distance [Original Archie Chisholm photograph: 1016; image © NMS].

the spoil heaps visible across the countryside today. The only significant mine workings on the islands are seen at Northton and Setteval, South Harris where large veins of feldspar were worked for their potash content during the 1940s.[9] What are visible though are large quarry scars in the mountainsides from place to place where the rocks have been extracted relatively recently to provide hardcore for the construction of roads and causeways.

Fig. 4.2: View of Loch Portain looking west showing typical landscape of North Uist with ice-fashioned rounded hills in the background [*Cairt Phostail* series postcard: 2107].

The Effects of Ice

Notwithstanding the control of the ancient bedrock the final morphology of today's landscape was fashioned by ice relatively recently. Some 13,000 years ago ice sheets advanced across Scotland and the Hebrides. The significant glaciers were located in the Northern Highlands and the Outer Isles would have been at the periphery of the ice sheets. The ice eroded and smoothed the bedrock to produce the mostly rounded contours seen today (Figs. 4.1 & 4.2). Where higher tracts remained, such as North Harris, glaciers were able to develop and sculpted deep u-shaped valleys. The ice retreated about 8,000 years ago leaving behind rocks and debris from the glaciers and fine silts and sands as outwash from the melting ice (Fig. 4.3). As the ice retreated sea levels began to rise and the land rebounded in response to removing the weight of the ice – the present-day Minch would have formed at about this time.

Fig. 4.3: Glacial erratic (isolated boulder) at Creag Hastin, North Uist [*Cairt Phostail* series postcard: 2179].

Creag Hastin, North Uist. (Copyright.)

Development of the Landscape after the Ice Age

The barren landscape post-ice would have been quickly colonised by advancing vegetation – known initially (8,000–5,000 years ago) to have been birch, pine and hazel and more recently (after 5,000 years ago) alder, oak and elm.[10] It is doubtful that the Outer Isles would have supported a complete tree cover given the barren rock-strewn nature of much of the higher ground. Beneath the present day blanket peat bogs, however, there are tree stumps that provide evidence of a former forest cover that developed in a drier climatic interval. At about this time (the Late Neolithic, 5,000–3,000 years ago) the first people are known to have migrated to the area – presumably following the forests and their animals as a source of food. Eventually the forest would have been cleared by the newly migrant populations for fuel or eventually removed to facilitate agriculture, leaving the treeless landscape seen today.

Viewed from the west coasts there is an obvious two-fold division of the land into the mountain and the *machair*[11] (Figs. 4.4 & 4.5). The first is self explanatory and has been little influenced

Fig. 4.4: View across the *machair* at Balranald, North Uist [*Cairt Phostail* series postcard: 2180].

Fig. 4.5: Ploughing the 'white land' of the *machair*. Also seen in the background are lazy beds in the 'black land'. Unlocated, probably South Uist [Original Archie Chisholm photograph: 1413; image © NMS].

by people. The *machair* is unique to the Atlantic coasts of the islands and has been strongly influenced by agriculture. The sandy low-lying tracts fringing the west coasts of the islands developed in response to the reworking of the glacial outwash and shell debris by sea and wind during the period of fluctuating sea levels since the retreat of the ice. This results in two distinct soil belts of the *machair*: the 'white land' adjacent to the dunes comprising sand only and the 'black land' where the sand overlies the peat.

The 'white land' is easy to plough, but has needed to be continually improved by fertilising with seaweed. The richer 'black land' is not so easy to farm due to its steeper gradient and so tended to have been developed by digging 'lazy beds' dug by a special spade (*caschrom*) separated by drains generally running perpendicular to the contours. These are an obvious feature to the landscape in most coastal areas of the islands (Fig. 4.5). Between the *machair* and the mountain is a zone of rough grazing with peat overlying the boulder clay (glacial debris).

East coasts by contrast are very rocky without any *machair* development and have little potential for agriculture (Fig.4.6).

These rough coasts though offer shelter from Atlantic storms and the benefit of deep harbours. Traditionally the settlements depended on fishing and latterly the towns became ferry ports. Today fishing for the local market has all but disappeared – the prawns landed at Stockinish are exported to Barcelona and the only fresh fish available in Harris comes via a mobile shop from Stornoway.

The Landscape in the *Cairt Phostail* Series Postcards

Archie took a considerable number of landscape photographs, sometimes choosing quite formidable locations on top of hills and rocky outcrops to position his camera equipment. Many were used to produce some of the *Cairt Phostail* picture postcards.

The following images show a selection of landscapes from Archie's photographs featured in the *Cairt Phostail* series as seen in North Uist (Figs. 4.7–4.9), Barra (Fig. 4.10), Harris (Fig. 4.11) and South Uist (Fig. 4.12).

Fig. 4.6: Typical rocky coastline on the east coast of South Harris at Ru Vollarip (*Rudha Bhalaroip*) [*Cairt Phostail* series postcard: 2050].

Fig. 4.7: View of Lochmaddy taken from the top of the Lee, North Uist [*Cairt Phostail* series postcard: 2174; scan courtesy of Norman Hudson]

Fig. 4.8: View of Lochmaddy taken from low ground below the Lee, North Uist, Crogearraidh Mor prominent in the background [*Cairt Phostail* series postcard: 2173].

Fig. 4.9: View of the Lees taken from Flodaigh, North Uist [*Cairt Phostail* series postcard: 2175].

Fig. 4.10: Breakers at Halaman Bay, Barra, continuing the cycle of erosion and deposition along the coast [*Cairt Phostail* series postcard: 2601].

Fig. 4.11: View of sandy estuary at the North Ford, between North Uist and Benbecula [*Cairt Phostail* series postcard: 2203; scan courtesy of Norman Hudson].

Fig. 4.12: View of Loch Grosebay (actually Loch Chollaim) on the rocky east coast of South Harris [*Cairt Phostail* series postcard: 2023; scan courtesy of Norman Hudson].

Landscapes Then and Now in Photographs

The rocky Hebridean landscape is relatively unchanging – and certainly has shown very little change since Archie took his photographs. The only real physically noticeable changes are in the shifting sands and dunes next to the coasts with rocky outcrops buried and exposed on the beaches from year to year and the dunes in overall retreat; the latter partly due to the impact of tourists and motor vehicles. All the superficial change is due to the impact of people – the building of houses and roads.

The six pairs of photographs (Figs. 4.13–4.18) compare the scenes captured in some of Archie's photographs taken on Harris with present day images. Most are little changed. The most noticeable impact on the landscape are new roads on embankments with tarmac, and safety rails and the building of a social housing development as seen at Ardhasaig (Fig. 4.13). Elsewhere, only a few new bungalows replacing old crofter cottages are all that show the era in which the photographs were taken (Figs. 4.15 & 4.16).

Fig. 4.13A (below left): The Scaw (*Sgaoth Iosal*) seen from the Tarbert to Stornoway road at Ardhasaig. The road to the left goes to Huisinis [Original Archie Chisholm photograph: 1006; image © NMS].

Fig. 4.13B (above): The Scaw today showing the effects of human impact from the building of new roads and a social housing development [Photograph: Michael Cope].

Fig. 4.14A (right): View from northern end of Loch Langabhat, South Harris. [Original Archie Chisholm photograph: 1024; Chisholm family collection].
Fig. 4.14B (above): Loch Langabhat today – unchanged apart from water level [Photograph: Michael Cope].

Fig. 4.15A (right): South-eastern side of Loch Plocropol, South Harris [Original Archie Chisholm photograph: 1019; image © NMS].
Fig. 4.15A (above): Loch Plocropol today [Photograph Alastair Chisholm].

Fig. 4.16A (right): Loch Chollaim, Grosebay, South Harris [Original Archie Chisholm photograph: 1022; Chisholm family collection].
Fig. 4.16B (above): Loch Chollaim today [Photograph: Alastair Chisholm].

In Archie's time Loch Langabhat was actively managed by the Hebridean Sporting Association for fishing of salmon and trout to suit the needs of sportsmen (see Chapter 12). The water level in the contemporary view is slightly higher today reflecting the more active management of the water in connection with the needs of the newly established industrial fisheries (Fig. 4.14).

Fig. 4.17A: Pigeon Cave at the coast below Boirseam, South Harris [Original Archie Chisholm photograph: 1040; Chisholm family collection].

Fig. 4.17B: Pigeon Cave today [Photograph: Michael Cope].

Fig. 4.18A: The coast at Rodel, South Harris as seen from the departing steamer [Original Archie Chisholm photograph: 1049; image © NMS].

The view from the sea to Rodel is not much changed, but the steamer no longer departs from here (Fig. 4.18) and today the main ferry link from Harris to Skye sails from Tarbert to Uig. The hotel, where Archie certainly stayed when it was the Rodel Lodge, gradually fell into disrepair and was closed in 1970, continuing only as a public bar. It was, however, renovated in 2001 and began taking guests again.

Fig. 4.18B: The coast at Rodel today [Photograph: Michael Cope].

Chapter 5

ANTIQUITIES AND OTHER HISTORICAL SITES

Neolithic Monuments

The earliest people probably came to the Outer Isles in the third millennium BC – sometime between 5,000 and 4,000 years ago. These people did not know the use of metal and so their tools and buildings were made of wood and stone. There is no shortage of rock-strewn terrain in the islands and so a ready supply of suitable material was available to these early builders. Across the islands there are many examples of Neolithic megalithic monuments, including chambered cairns, stone circles and standing stones. Archie provides a photographic record of several of these monuments on North Uist.

The best known chambered cairn is the *Barpa* at Langash (*Langass*; Fig. 5.1). The mound of stones some 6 metres high covers several collapsed burial chambers, although no human remains have been found there. Erskine Beveridge, in *North Uist: Its Archaeology and Topography*,[8] describes some excavations at the site that found evidence of burnt burials together with flints, arrowheads, patterned pottery and a disc of talc, this shaped and pierced as if an item of jewellery. The structure was designated as a scheduled monument in 1934 and in 2000 Historic Environment Scotland amended the schedule to include a greater surrounding area of archaeological significance;[12] since 1990 the monument has been under the ownership of the North Uist Estate Trust.

About a kilometre to the southeast of the *Barpa*, overlooking Loch Langais, is a stone circle known locally as *Pobull Fhinn* (Fionn's People) or *Sòrnach a' Phobaill* (the Fireplace of the

Fig. 5.1A (right): The *Barpa* at Langash (*Langass*), North Uist [*Cairt Phostail* series postcard: 2192].
Fig. 5.1B (above): The *Barpa* today, now designated as a scheduled monument [Photograph: Michael Cope].

Fig. 5.2A (right): Ancient stone circle (*Pobull Fhinn* or *Sòrnach a' Phobaill*) above Loch Langais, North Uist [*Cairt Phostail* series postcard: 2191; scan courtesy of Norman Hudson].
Fig. 5.2B (above): The stone circle today [Photograph: Michael Cope].

People), probably named after the legendary Gaelic hero *Fionn mac Cumhaill* known in English as Finn or Fingal (Fig. 5.2).[13] Of the several stone circles on the island, *Pobull Fhinn* is the most conspicuous. It possibly dates from the second millennium BC. The 'circle', measures about 40 metres by 30 metres. At least two dozen stones can be counted and at the east side is a tall single stone, and there are two fallen slabs beyond the western edge.

Clach a Che and Dun, Claddach-Kirkibost, North Uist. (Copyright).

Fig. 5.3A (left): The *Clach a Che* standing stone and dun, Claddach-Kirkibost, North Uist [*Cairt Phostail* series postcard: 2181].
Fig. 5.3B (above): The standing stone and dun today [Photograph: Michael Cope].

The purpose of the circle is unknown, but presumably had some ritual significance.

A well preserved standing stone known as *Clach Mhor a' Che* (the great stone of Che) is located on the shore at Claddach Kyles overlooking Kirkibost Island (Fig. 5.3).[14] The stone stands 2.7m high, is 1.2m wide and 0.3m thick. It probably dates from between the first and third millennium BC. Erskine Beveridge suggested that the stone was the subject of several local legends and perhaps that it marks the site of a battle. To the left of the picture are the possible remains of a dun or fort. A similar stone known as *Chladh Maelrubha*, also photographed by Archie, can be seen on Berneray at the top of Beinn a' Chlaidh.

Medieval Fortified Sites

Crannogs are artificial islets constructed in lochs in many parts of Scotland. They served as dwelling sites that were easily defended, usually with the only access being by boat or a causeway. Many were further strengthened for defence with the construction of duns (or forts) on the artificial foundations.

Fig. 5.4A (right): *Dun Aonghais*, near Ahmore, North Uist [*Cairt Phostail* series postcard: 2105].
Fig. 5.4B (above): The dun and loch today; the reed beds have expanded across the loch [Photograph: Michael Cope].

Fig. 5.5A (right): *Dun Mhicleoid* on Loch Tangasdall, Barra [*Cairt Phostail* series postcard: 2602].
Fig. 5.5B (above): The dun and loch today [Photograph: Michael Cope].

Crannogs are generally thought to date from the Late Bronze Age to the Iron Age (c.1250 BC to 43 AD). New research by the University of Reading[15] has shown that these structures might be considerably older, as Neolithic pottery has been recovered from the loch floors near several crannogs in Lewis. Many sites have a long history of settlement with some being occupied and fortified in medieval times as late as the 16th century. Archie

Fig. 5.6A (left): Ruins of dun, Borve, Benbecula [*Cairt Phostail* series postcard: 2304A].
Fig. 5.6B (above): Ruins of dun at Borve today [Photograph: Alastair. Chisholm].

photographed two such sites.

The first is *Dun Aonghuis* (translated as the fort of Angus), located in Loch Aonghuis on North Uist near the coastal village of Ahmore(Fig. 5.4).[16] The fort sits on an artificial foundation approximately 30 metres in diameter, connected to the bank by a causeway. Erskine Beveridge states that the fort was occupied in the 16th century by *Aonghus Fionn* (Angus the Fair) who came from Skye to avenge his father's death sometime after 1510.

The second is the *Dun Mhic Leoid* in Loch Tangasdail on Barra (Fig. 5.5). This dates from the mid-15th century and according to the archaeological notes on the Canmore website[17] the fort is an unvaulted tower originally of three stories with traces of a substantial roundhouse underlying the medieval tower. There are also traces of a submerged causeway to the south side of the loch. There is no apparent local history or tradition concerning the structure.

Some duns were built on natural sites and not always surrounded by water. *Dun Borve* (also known as Castle Wearie or Borve Castle) on Benbecula[18] (Fig. 5.6) is believed to have been built by Amy MacRuairi, the first wife of John of Islay, chief of Clan Donald. Following John divorcing Amy in order to marry into

Fig. 5.7: Ruins of dun (*Caisteal a' Bhreabadair*), Na Stachan Dubha, Sound of Barra [*Cairt Phostail* series postcard: 2507].

Fig. 5.8: Kisimul Castle, Castlebay, Barra seen from Gearrygall [Original Archie Chisholm photograph: 1615A; image © NMS].

and align himself with the House of Stewart, Amy built several chapels and two castles, including Dun Borve in Benbecula. The dun is thought to have been built between 1344 and 1363, and became the seat of Clan Ranald. Although now sadly in ruins, the structure is likely to have been three stories tall. It was occupied by the Macdonalds of Benbecula until the early 17th century.

By contrast two sites photographed further south had used rocky outcrops in the sea as a natural fortification.

Weaver's Castle (*Caisteal a' Bhreabadair*) situated on a sea stack south of Eriskay (Fig. 5.7) is described in the Canmore record[19] as: a mortared rubble ruin of a tower of uncertain date, once a stronghold of the MacNeils. Later it was the home of the notorious pirate wrecker Breabadair Stache (weaver being a corruption of riever). He and most of his family were eventually slain by soldiers. The steep cliffs on all sides make this a very secure site.

Kisimul Castle (*Caisteal Chiosmuil*) which sits on a rocky islet at Castlebay, Barra also falls into this category (Fig. 5.8). This building's history is discussed and illustrated more fully in Chapter 9 (see Figs. 9.13 to 9.15).

Ecclesiastical Sites

The *Teampull na Trionaid* (or Trinity Temple) at Carinish on North Uist is probably the best known of the medieval ecclesiastical monuments in the Outer Isles (Fig. 5.9). According to the Canmore record[20] the structure has an uncertain early history but was possibly built c.1200, and it was probably enlarged in the late 14th century when Amy MacRuari (see above) developed it into

Fig. 5.9A (left): Trinity Temple, Carinish, North Uist [*Cairt Phostail* series postcard: 2196].
Fig. 5.9B (above): Trinity Temple, today [Photograph: Alastair Chisholm].

Cille-Chalumcille, Benbecula. (Copyright)

Fig. 5.10A (right): *Cille Chalumcille*, near Balivanich, Benbecula [*Cairt Phostail* series postcard: 2301; scan courtesy of Norman Hudson]. Fig. 5.10B (above): *Cille Chalumcille* today [Photograph: Michael Cope].

an important seat of learning. Following further reconstruction in the 16th century, the *Teampull* was still used for public worship as late as 1728. A major restoration was carried out in 2011 using traditional masonry techniques. Archaeological excavations undertaken at the same time found nothing other than 19th century human and animal bones.

The ruined *Teampull Chalumcille* or Chapel of St Columba, near Balivanich (*Baile Mhanaich*) on the Island of Benbecula[21] (Fig. 5.10) would once have stood on a small promontory on the shore of Loch na Cille. The loch has since been drained, making access to the ruin across boggy ground quite difficult. The earliest parts of the ruin may date from the time of St Columba himself (c.521–597). The east end probably dates to the end of the 14th century and may have been built by Amy MacRuairi.

St Clement's church at Rodel on Harris (Fig. 5.11) has a rich history and this is best described in the books of Bill Lawson – *Harris in History and Legend*[22] and *St Clement's Church at Rodel*.[23] It seems that the church was built around 1520 for the chiefs of the MacLeods of Harris who lived in Dunvegan on Skye. It may have been constructed on an earlier Celtic site, but there is no firm evidence for this. Dean Donald Monro, writing in 1549,

Fig. 5.11A (left): St Clement's Church at Rodel, South Harris [Original Archie Chisholm photograph: 1042; image © NMS].
Fig. 5.11B (above): St Clement's Church today [Photograph: Alastair Chisholm].

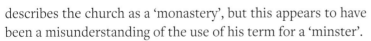

Fig. 5.12A (left): Tomb of Alasdair Crotach, St Clement's, Rodel, South Harris [*Cairt Phostail* series postcard: 2044].
Fig. 5.12B (above): Tomb of Alasdair Crotach today [Photograph: Michael Cope].

describes the church as a 'monastery', but this appears to have been a misunderstanding of the use of his term for a 'minster'.

The church has undergone several reconstructions after falling into disrepair in about 1560. It was rescued in 1784 by Captain Alexander MacLeod after he purchased the Harris estate from his cousin Norman MacLeod, the clan chief at the time. Shortly after the restoration the building was damaged by a fire and had to be rebuilt again in 1787. The rebuilding work was never fully completed due to the death of Captain MacLeod in 1790. Again the church fell into disrepair to the extent that in the 19th century it was being used as a cattle byre. The last restoration of St Clement's was in 1873 by the Countess of Dunmore, the owner of South Harris at the time.

St Clement's is notable for containing the wall tombs of Alasdair Crotach (Alexander MacLeod) and William MacLeod, father and son, 8th and 9th chiefs of Clan MacLeod of Harris and Dunvegan. The tomb of Alasdair Crotach is noted for its detailed biblical carvings (Fig. 5.12) and was constructed in 1528 during his lifetime – he died in 1547. William also had his tomb constructed while he was still living in 1539. Both tombs depict the chiefs dressed in mail and bearing a sword, depicting a life of warfare, but it is thought that Alasdair ended his life in religious seclusion at Rodel.

Bonnie Prince Charlie's Landing Place

The story of the landing of Charles Edward Stuart (Bonnie Prince Charlie) on Eriskay and his subsequent journey to the Scottish mainland on the eve of the 1745 Jacobite rebellion is well known. The Prince's frigate, the *Du Teillay*, was caught in a bad storm approaching Barra on 23rd July 1745. The frigate was also being pursued by the British navy and circumstances led to the Prince's party putting ashore further north on the sheltered beach south of Bala on Eriskay – today known as Prince Charlie's Beach (*Coilleag a' Phrionnsa*). He spent what he described as 'a very wet dirty night' in a crude hut about a mile north of the beach, in what is now the village of Bala (*Am Baile*). The following night the *Du Teillay* set sail for Glenfinnan on the mainland.

Eriskay's part in Bonnie Prince Charlie's story is quite brief, but that did not stop interest in the events there developing in

Fig. 5.13: Bala, Eriskay where Prince Charlie first slept in Britain [*Cairt Phostail* series postcard: 2503A].

Fig. 5.14: Eriskay, the spot where Prince Charlie first landed in Britain for the '45 [*Cairt Phostail* series postcard: 2504A].

Fig. 5.15: Prince Charlie's first landing-place in Britain for the '45 [*Cairt Phostail* series postcard: 2505A].

subsequent years. By Archie's time there was even scope for him to tap into the burgeoning tourist industry with a special edition of the *Cairt Phostail* series. There were four cards produced with colour tints of Bala village and the landing place (Figs. 5.13–5.16); these views were also originally produced in a black and white edition. It is believed that the person seen pointing out the beach in Figs. 5.14 and 5.15 is Father Allan MacDonald, the famous Catholic priest and scholar of Eriskay.

After the death of her husband Colonel Gordon, Lady Cathcart became the owner of Eriskay. In 1900 she had the hut where Prince Charlie stayed that first night demolished, so as to remove a focal point for any lingering popular feelings for his cause, and against her, from the local population. The stones were used to build a new house – this is the red-roofed house in Archie's photograph (Fig 5.16). It still has the red roof clearly visible in today's photograph, albeit in extended form, but all the surrounding thatched blackhouses have been demolished (Fig. 5.17). The overgrown rubble that was the foundations of the hut can still be seen about 100 metres away on the opposite side of the road (Fig. 5.18).

Fig. 5.16: In Bala, Eriskay, where Prince Charlie slept first night in Britain [*Cairt Phostail* series postcard: 2506].

In Bala, Eriskay, where Prince Charlie slept first night in Britain. (Copyright)

Fig. 5.17: Aerial view of Bala today with the house, left centre, built from the remains of Prince Charlie's shelter clearly distinguished by its red roof [Photograph: Michael Cope].

Fig. 5.18: Foundation rubble of hut used to shelter Prince Charlie [Photograph: Michael Cope].

Prince Charlie's Beach is still a popular tourist destination today and a cairn was erected in the dunes behind the beach by the children of Eriskay School in 1995 to commemorate the 250th anniversary of the landing.

Fig. 6.1: Crofter's house, Plocropol, South Harris [Original Archie Chisholm photograph: 1020; image © NMS].

Chapter 6

Crofting Communities

The Origins of Crofting

Crofting as a distinct type of land tenure and practice of agriculture is unique to the Hebridean islands and the northwest Scottish mainland. Its origins are to be found in the transition of traditional clan systems of support into a landlord and tenant transaction which occurred in the mid 18th century following the subjugation of the Highlands after 1746. As Samuel Johnson commented in his account of *A Journey to the Western Islands of Scotland* (1775),[24] the Highland chiefs had:

> already lost much of their influence; and as they gradually degenerate from patriarchal rulers to rapacious landlords, they will divest themselves of the little that remains.

By 1800 those clansmen who had not emigrated to North America were converted into crofters – tenants who would pay rent. The means whereby a tenant farmer could make a living and provide for their families came to an end as landlords raised rents to levels that could not be paid by earnings from the croft alone. Crofters were therefore forced into other labour, usually working for their landlords. In the Outer Isles this income gap was conveniently filled by the development of the kelping industry – the extraction of alkalis from gathered seaweed for use in glass and soap manufacture. It provided employment and wages for the crofters, albeit just sufficient to keep up payment of their rents, and was highly profitable for the landlords. This economic system foundered in the early 1800s as new sources of alkalis came onto the market and kelp prices collapsed. Faced with a reduction in their incomes the landowners turned to a new system of population and agricultural management known collectively as the 'clearances'.

The clearances, especially in the Hebrides, were the means whereby landlords replaced kelping as a source of income with more profitable sheep rearing. This involved the appropriation of better quality crofting land to be let as much larger farms to new incoming farmers able to pay a higher rent. The remaining crofting population was forced into ever smaller plots of marginal land. These new crofts were not of sufficient size or quality to generate the rentals asked by the landlords and so the crofting population had to endure more hardship or be forced to emigrate, either to the south of the country or overseas. In the 1860s and 1870s even sheep were not providing the revenue required by the land owners and there was a widespread shift of converting sheep pasture to deer forests, but of course this did not provide any more land to the crofters. The growth of sporting estates and sports tourism is described more fully in Chapter 12.

A great deal has been written about the clearances, especially the ensuing emigration, and they are often presented as an

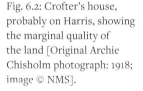

Fig. 6.2: Crofter's house, probably on Harris, showing the marginal quality of the land [Original Archie Chisholm photograph: 1918; image © NMS].

economic *necessity* to enable landowners to deal with the pressures arising from a growing population unable to be supported by the diminishing amount of available land. In *The Making of the Crofting Community*[25] James Hunter makes the case for the alternative viewpoint, that the clearances were an economic *choice* made by landowners simply to increase the profitability of their estates. The end result of this policy was that through the 19th century crofters' living conditions became increasingly intolerable. Any effort to improve their land or living conditions was met with increases in rent, while the threat of eviction and destitution was ever present.

The Landowners

The Outer Isles were the domain of the Lord of the Isles until the 15th century when the estates on the various islands were granted to a number of clan chiefs – in the case of the Long Island, the Macleods of Harris, the Macdonalds of Sleat, the Macdonalds of Clan Ranald and the Clan Macneil. By the middle of the 19th century all of these former clan ownerships had been sold to a new cohort of owners with no historical connection to the land who vigorously pursued the practice of land clearances as a means of seeking a return on their investments. It is interesting to catalogue who owned what at the time Archie was in the islands.

Harris was purchased by the 5th Earl of Dunmore from Alexander Norman Macleod in 1834 for £60,000. Ownership was passed down through the family and was in the hands of the 7th Earl (Charles Adolphus Murray, 1841–1907) by the time of Archie's arrival. Charles relinquished the North Harris estate to his bankers, the Scott family, in lieu of debts in 1868. The Scott family maintained ownership of the estate until after WW1. The remaining South Harris estate passed to the 8th Earl (Alexander Edward Murray, 1871–1962) in 1907. Much of Harris is today in the ownership of a number of community trusts which purchased

Fig. 6.3: Cottar's house at Finsbay, Harris, taken in 1904 [Original Archie Chisholm photograph: 1034; image © NMS].

Fig. 6.4: Crofters' houses at Kentangval, Barra, taken in 1901 [Original Archie Chisholm photograph: 1605; image © NMS].

Fig. 6.5: Crofter family and their cow at Claddach Illeray, North Uist, taken in 1897 [Original Archie Chisholm photograph: 1184; image © NMS].

various parts of the island from 2003 onwards.

North Uist was purchased from the Macdonalds of Sleat in 1855 by the 3rd Baronet of Morpeth (Sir John William Prowlett Campbell-Orde, 1827–1897). As described in Chapter 2, his behaviour towards his tenants led to direct conflict with Archie as both a solicitor and Procurator Fiscal in Lochmaddy in the 1890s. Archie's difficulties were resolved with the succession of the 4th Baronet (Sir Arthur John Campbell-Orde, 1865–1933) in 1897. Today the island is owned by the Granville family through the North Uist Estate Trust.

South Uist, Benbecula and Eriskay were originally owned by the Macdonalds of Clan Ranald and sold to Lieutenant Colonel John Gordon of Cluny in 1837 (Eriskay in 1841). Known as the 'most heartless of the landowners' in the Outer Isles, he died in 1858 and the estates passed to his illegitimate son, Captain John Gordon (1820?–1878), after considerable legal wrangles. Captain Gordon married Emily Pringle in 1865 and she inherited the estates on his death in 1878. She later married Sir Reginald Cathcart in 1880 and became Lady Cathcart, continuing to own the estates for all of Archie's time on the islands – she died in 1932 having only visited the island once. The South Uist, Benbecula and Eriskay estates were purchased in 2006 by the community owned company Sealladh na Beinne Mòire.

Barra was originally granted to the Clan Macneil and became part of Colonel John Gordon's estates when sold to him in 1838. Subsequently Barra also passed into Lady Cathcart's ownership. The island returned to Macneil ownership in 1937 when it was bought by Robert Lister Macneil, a clan descendant living in America and working as an architect. Under his ownership Kisimul Castle at Castlebay was restored in a project completed in 1970. The Barra estate was transferred to the Scottish Government in 2003. None of the landowners of the day appear in any of Archie's known photographs.

The Highland Land War 1881–1896

James Hunter[25] provides an excellent account of these events which occurred during the first half of Archie's tenure in Lochmaddy. I have selected some incidents from this conflict, mostly relating to Archie's area of jurisdiction, of which it is possible he would have had quite some knowledge as a local law officer at the time.

Archie arrived in Lochmaddy in 1881 at a time of considerable unrest in the Hebridean crofting community. In 1881 harvests failed and the plight of crofters became as abject as it had been in the times of the potato blights of the 1840s and 1850s. Matters first came to a head on Skye in 1882 when crofters undertook rent strikes, moved their stock onto sheep pastures and made land seizures. Concerned with the growing unrest, the government eventually set up a Royal Commission in 1883 (the Napier Commission) to 'inquire into the condition of the crofters and cottars in the Highlands and Islands of Scotland'. The crofters themselves set up their own representative movement in 1883; known as the Highland Land Law Reform Association (later the Highland Land League), it had a paid-up membership of about 5,000 by 1884.

Rent strikes and land occupations spread throughout the Long Island. On Lewis farm fences were destroyed and boulders placed on roads to harass farmers and factors. In North Uist crofters pegged out new 'crofts' on sheep farms at Balelone and Balranald. In South Uist lands of Ormacleit farm were occupied and fertilised with seaweed ready for new cultivation; telegraph wires were also cut. Attempts to bring perpetrators to justice were met with angry mobs attacking sheriff officers. As a result armed marines were dispatched to Skye and Lewis to act as escorts to police attempting to make arrests.

Against this background of land agitation, the conclusions of the Napier Commission led to the implementation of the

Fig. 6.6: Crofters' houses and horse and cart at Claddach Illeray, North Uist, taken in 1897; note the stack of peats outside [Original Archie Chisholm photograph: 1185; image © NMS].

Fig. 6.7: Crofters' houses and family, unlocated, probably North Uist, taken in 1903 [Original Archie Chisholm photograph: 1925; image © NMS].

Crofters' Act in 1886 which at least addressed the crofters' principal grievances: providing them with security of tenure on their crofts, setting fair rents and compensating them for improvements on relinquishing their tenancies. But this was not the end of unrest as the Act did nothing for the landless cottars, sub-tenants of crofters, who eked out a still miserable existence. As a result there were continued land occupations and

Fig. 6.8A (right): Scadabay, Harris, undated c.1900 [Original Archie Chisholm photograph: 1021; image © NMS].
Fig. 6.8B (above): Scadabay, Harris today [Photograph: Alastair Chisholm].

confrontations with the authorities. In January 1888 the stock from two farms, at Aignish and Melbost on Lewis were driven into the grounds of Lady Matheson's residence at Stornoway Castle. In the confrontation following the reading of the Riot Act several hundred crofters and cottars faced off with police constables, soldiers from the Royal Scots and marines. Archie's opposite number, the Procurator Fiscal of Stornoway, while observing the scene, revolver in hand, was assaulted. Whether he and Archie ever met to discuss the events is not known!

Iin Harris crofters and cottars were petitioning factors and landlords for more land to be made available. Cottars in South Uist resolved that they would not 'let ourselves or our families starve as long as there is cultivable land growing under sheep in Uist, or as long as there is anything in Uist that we can lay our hands upon to prevent such starvation'. The Sheriff-Substitute at Lochmaddy reported of the situation:

> The disturbances in Lewis have had a very serious effect; they are of course, much talked of, and the conduct of the people applauded, and opinions held and expressed that it would be well to follow suit.

Fig. 6.9A (left): Ruisgarry Quay, Berneray, undated c.1900 [Original Archie Chisholm photograph: 1101; image © NMS].
Fig. 6.9B (above): Ruisgarry Quay, Berneray today [Photograph: Alastair Chisholm].

Fig. 6.10A (left): Hougarry, North Uist, undated c.1900 [*Cairt Phostail* series postcard; 2104].
Fig. 6.10B (above): Hougarry, North Uist today [Photograph: Alastair Chisholm].

But, in Harris, the Uists and Barra there were no actual land seizures at this time. This may explain the mention in Archie's Lochmaddy leaving presentation that he had a role in keeping troops out of his part of the Long Island – the authorities at Lochmaddy having some autonomy to defuse the situation

Fig. 6.11A (right): Sowing grain at Obbe, Harris, May 1904 [Original Archie Chisholm photograph: 1039; image © NMS].
Fig. 6.11B (above): The scene today showing the new road to the ferry terminal [Photograph: Michael Cope].

compared with the more heavy-handed approach adopted by their opposite numbers in Portree and Stornoway. Also Archie's suggestion that the people themselves averted the deployment of the military was perhaps because of their less aggressive actions compared with those in Lewis and Skye.

Progress on the distribution of new land began to be made with the establishment in 1897 of the Congested Districts Board, which was empowered to improve agricultural conditions and make land purchases for resettlement of crofters and cottars. Nevertheless, there was still land agitation in the Long Island in the early years of the 20th century. In September 1900 cottars occupied Northbay Farm on Barra and the adjacent island of Vatersay. In 1901 cottars on South Uist petitioned the Board for land at Ormacleit and Bornish farms. Similarly cottars on North Uist petitioned the Board to purchase land from the Campbell-Orde Estate. Eventually the Board was able to purchase about 50 plots on Vatersay from Lady Cathcart for £600. In 1908, after more occupations of Vatersay and the prosecution and imprisonment of some of those concerned, the Board negotiated the purchase of the entirety of Vatersay for £6,250. In both of these transactions

Fig. 6.12A (left): Donald and Malcolm MacAskill, cottars from Obbe, cutting peats at Loch na Moracha, Steisebhat, Harris, May 1904 [Original Archie Chisholm photograph: 1035; image © NMS].
Fig. 6.12B (above): Old peat banks at Loch na Moracha, Steisebhat, Harris, now largely overgrown [Photograph: Michael Cope].

it was considered that Lady Cathcart received far more than the real value of the land.

With continuing threats of land raids into the second decade of the 1900s and the seeming failure of the Congested Districts Board to achieve the amount of resettlement required, the Board of Agriculture for Scotland was established in 1912 as a successor organisation. It was to the former body that Thomas

Fig. 6.13: Building a haystack, unlocated and undated, probably North Uist c.1900 [Original Archie Chisholm photograph: 1909; image © NMS].

Wilson, Archie's former legal partner, was appointed as factor and law agent in 1911.[4] Although better resourced than its predecessor, it was not until after WW1, following the Land Settlement (Scotland) Act in 1919, some time after Archie had returned to Inverness, that the Board of Agriculture was provided with sufficient funds to make enough land purchases to have a significant impact on the crofter and cottar communities. In this later period Thomas Wilson became its Senior Sub-Commissioner for Smallholdings until his retirement in 1933.

Archie's Photographs of Crofting Communities

Most of Archie's photographs of crofting communities were taken after the Land War in the late 1890s and early 1900s, but as is apparent the conditions of the crofters and cottars were far from ideal, the main upturn in their fortunes coming after he left Lochmaddy. The conditions prevailing in 1889 are vividly described by F. G. Rea in his memoir *A School in South Uist: Reminiscences of a Hebridean School Master 1890–1913*.[26] On his arrival in South Uist, he recounts:

> I shall not forget the shock I had, after a mile or so searching the road left and right for dwelling houses and only seeing in the fast failing light, a few what looked to be large isolated heaps of stones or earth, lying well back some hundred yards or so from the road we were traversing. I burst out: 'But where are the houses?' Pointing to one of the black-looking heaps I had noticed, my conductor replied: 'Those are the houses!'

Fig. 6.14: Milking a cow, unlocated and undated, probably North Uist c.1900 [Original Archie Chisholm photograph: 1904; image © NMS].

Fig. 6.15: Shearing sheep, probably Harris, c.1900 [Original Archie Chisholm photograph: 1908; image © NMS].

These were typical crofters' 'blackhouses', low constructions of rough stones with straw or heather roofs with a single access door, sometimes with a small window and sometimes a vent for the peat fire that burned continually. One end of the house served as a living and sleeping area for the family and the other sheltered their animals. Some examples from Harris, North Uist and Barra are shown in Figs. 6.1–6.7.

The crofters' houses were grouped into townships – collections of smallholdings, each with its own few hectares of pasture and arable land and a common tract of unimproved upland grazing. It was the restriction of the historical rights to the common grazing areas that led to the initial unrest in Skye. The members of the township would collaborate on common tasks, such as maintaining the common pasture, digging and collecting the peat, and fishing. Today the township is a legal entity recognised by the Crofters Commission. Several townships are featured in Archie's photographs; some taken on Harris, Berneray and North Uist are shown as Figs. 6.8–6.10.

Day-to-day crofting tasks and collective endeavours were also captured in Archie's photographs, such as planting and harvesting grain (Fig. 6.11), cutting peats (Fig. 6.12; although in this example the work is being carried out by cottars), collecting and storing fodder (Fig. 6.13), milking cattle (Fig. 6.14) and shearing sheep (Fig. 6.15). Fishing was another essential activity for crofters to supplement their income and this is dealt with in more detail in Chapter 11.

There were certainly some improvements in crofters' lives and conditions during Archie's time at Lochmaddy, especially after 1897 when most of his photographs were taken. These improvements are captured in one rather idyllic composition showing a new crofters' homestead on (North?) Uist (Fig. 6.16) – perhaps built as the result of actions of the Congested Districts Board?

Picturesque Uist, a New Crofter's Homestead. (Copyright).

Fig. 6.16: Picturesque Uist, a New Crofter's Homestead [*Cairt Phostail* series postcard: 2907].

Fig. 6.17A (top): Two men (bailiffs?) emptying the contents of a blackhouse at Lochmaddy, c.1900 [Original Archie Chisholm photograph: 1146; image © NMS]. Fig. 6.17B (above): The scene today, the house has been demolished [Photograph: Alastair Chisholm].

The Eviction Photographs

The somewhat controversial eviction scene photographs come mostly from the lantern slides provided by Margaret Paterson, although a few duplicate images are in the Scottish Life Archive Cathcart Collection and from prints provided by Norman Johnson of Lochmaddy.

These photographs depict at least two different events. The first is certainly in Lochmaddy with the scene located west of the main road, behind the Old Court House (Fig. 6.17) – too good an opportunity for Archie to miss! The house being emptied has since been demolished. Whether this is a true eviction or a removal

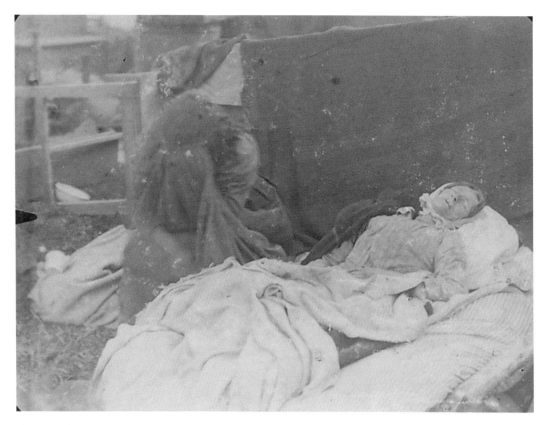

Fig. 6.18: Sick woman lying down and another woman apparently weeping at the eviction scene shown in Fig. 6.17A; these may be Mary MacDermid and her niece Kate [Original Archie Chisholm photograph reproduced from lantern slide collection of Margaret Paterson: 1930].

due to rehousing is not known, but that Archie was aware of the event suggests that there is some legal basis for the process of which, as Procurator Fiscal, he would have known. Also, given his involvement in eviction proceedings with Sir John Campbell-Orde, the situation was no doubt of particular interest to him.

There are two other photographs showing apparently sick or distressed women and children sitting on the ground with the bailiff close by going about his business (Figs. 6.18 & 6.19). Bill Lawson in his book *North Uist in History and Legend*[27] states that the old woman in the scene above is Mary MacDermid and that she was being removed from the house as it was to be demolished to allow extension of the Court House. What

Fig. 6.19: Distressed women and children at an eviction scene. It is not certain if this is the same event as shown in Fig. 6.17A [Original Archie Chisholm photograph reproduced from lantern slide collection of Margaret Paterson: 1931].

is clear is that in Fig. 6.17A the terraced wall surrounding the Court House is in the same position as it is today, so an extension was never built over the site of the house; a small lean-to structure, however, has since been built against the Court House wall (Fig. 6.17B).

There is a further set of photographs (Figs. 6.20–6.22) relating to another eviction which Bill Lawson notes are related to the removal of Donald MacKiggan's family for a road widening scheme. We have been unable to locate this scene.

It is plain that none of these events are related to the clearances and we are not aware that this claim was ever made by Archie. While it is possible that some of the scenes may

Figs. 6.20–6.22: Unlocated
eviction scenes, possibly of
Donald MacKiggan's family
[Original Archie Chisholm
photographs reproduced
from lantern slide collection
of Margaret Paterson: 1936,
1934, 1932].

have been staged for the camera, what Archie was doing here was documenting the fact that evictions of tenants were still occurring for whatever reason some time after the protections of the Crofters' Act had been implemented. The fact that the Campbell-Orde estate was involved surely would have stirred his interest in the events and the taking of the photographs may well have inflamed the enmity between Sir John and Archie.

Chapter 7

Transport and Communications

In Archie's day the only way to reach the Outer Isles was by sea, usually by a commercial steamer service from Wester Ross for Lewis, from Skye for Harris and North Uist, and from Glasgow or Oban for the southern isles. These late 19th to earliest 20th century steamer services were the forerunners of today's CalMac car ferries and many of the routes are little changed. A snapshot of these steamer routes in 1908 is provided by Bartholomew's map of the Western Isles Routes (Fig. 7.1).

The steamer routes themselves had their origins in the regular mail packet services established by estate owners in order to communicate with their factors and others on their island estates – primarily to support their business interests. The first of these services were established in the mid 18th century and from their inception the estate owners sought subsidies from the General Post Office on the basis that these ships were carrying the Queen's mails. When the subsidies were not sufficient to cover the running costs of the services, the owners sometimes suspended or withdrew the packets until subsidies were improved; vessels, routes and connections changed constantly and shipwrecks were common in the treacherous waters of the Minch. A detailed account of these early packet and mail steamer routes is given by James A. Mackay in his booklets *Islands Postal History Series, Volumes 1, 2 & 3*.[28, 29, 30] His accounts of the steamer services relating to Harris, the Uists and Barra provide a useful background for the period Archie was in Lochmaddy (1881 to 1913).

By the 1860s the Outer Hebrides as a whole came into regular communication with the mainland for the first time with the opening of new steamship routes operated by Martin Orme

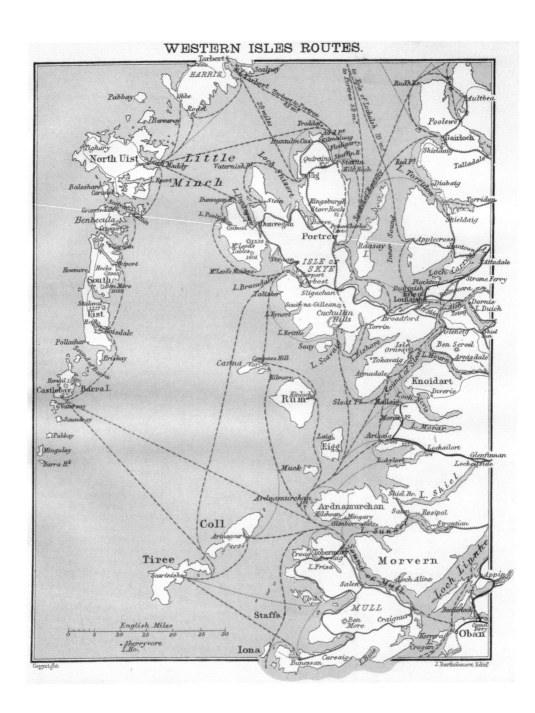

between Glasgow, the Hebrides and Wester Ross (Glasgow-Oban-Mull-Coll-Tiree-Lochboisdale-Lochmaddy-Tarbert-Ullapool-Lochinver). An additional service was introduced in 1872 (Glasgow-Oban-Quinish-Dunvegan-Uig-Tarbert-Rodel (later Obbe)-Lochmaddy-Kallin-Lochboisdale-Barra). The route was operated from 1875 by the SS *Dunara Castle*, a vessel which was eventually to assist in the evacuation of St Kilda in August 1930.

In 1886 both North Uist and Harris were connected by a new route from Skye operated daily by the MacBrayne steamers *Handa*, *Staffa* and *Lochiel*. (Portree-Tarbert-Lochmaddy-Dunvegan; the *Lochiel* ran aground at Portree in 1907 and, being broken up, was succeeded on the route by the *Lapwing*). A connecting service from Portree to the railhead at Stromeferry (see Fig. 3.2) is listed in the MacBrayne's guide of 1884 as departing daily July to October and three times weekly in winter – the fare was 10s return and 6s 8d single.[31] This would probably have been the service and ship which first brought Archie to Lochmaddy. In the 1880s and 1890s MacBrayne also maintained daily connections from Oban to Barra, South Uist and Benbecula continuing to Lochmaddy and Dunvegan with the steamers

Fig. 7.1 (facing page): Steamer routes in the Western Isles in 1908. By this time the mainland railhead can be seen to have extended to Kyle of Lochalsh [Image © Antiqua Print Gallery / Alamy Stock Photo].

Fig. 7.2A (left): Rodel Hotel, port and jetty [Original Archie Chisholm photograph: 1048; image © NMS].
Fig. 7.2B (above): Rodel today [Photograph: Alastair Chisholm].

Fig. 7.3A (right): Arrival of a steamer at Lochmaddy; from the funnel markings it is probably not one of the MacBrayne fleet [Original Archie Chisholm photograph: 1164; image © NMS].

Fig. 7.3B (above): A very different scene today with the arrival of the CalMac ferry *Clansman* at Lochmaddy Pier [Photograph: Michael Cope].

Clydesdale and *Flowerdale*. By 1898 there was an additional stop for the route between Lochmaddy and Tarbert at Rodel (Fig. 7.2). Writing in 1902 in her book *Outer Isles*,[32] Ada Goodrich-Freer describes her port of call there:

> As there is no pier one has to row to the shore in a small boat,
> but except in bad weather when the boat is more than usually

Fig. 7.4A (right): Steamer arriving at Tarbert, probably one of MacBrayne's fleet [*Cairt Phostail* series postcard: 2012].

Fig. 7.4B (above): CalMac ferry *Hebrides* approaching the terminal at Tarbert today [Photograph: Michael Cope].

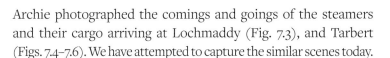

Fig. 7.5A (left): Steamer berthed at Tarbert Pier, looking east [*Cairt Phostail* series postcard: 2013; scan courtesy of Norman Hudson]. Fig. 7.5B (above): Today's foot passenger berth at the Tarbert terminal; the overall layout has not much changed in a hundred years [Photograph: Michael Cope].

crowded with cattle and stores, it is easy enough, especially if the tide admits of the choice of a convenient landing place. There is a little coffee house at Obbe, three miles away, where one can spend the night if necessary, as of course the mail steamer leaves at once and may not return for some days.

Archie photographed the comings and goings of the steamers and their cargo arriving at Lochmaddy (Fig. 7.3), and Tarbert (Figs. 7.4–7.6). We have attempted to capture the similar scenes today.

Getting Around the Islands

When Archie arrived in Lochmaddy there would have been no motorised transport. There were, however, roads between the major centres, classed as 'Secondary (Good)' on the Bartholomew's half-inch maps of 1902–1904. Roads between villages were classed as 'Passable', with the cautionary note that these were not recommended for cyclists! The roads themselves were made from compacted rocks and earth – there was no tarmac in use on the islands at that time. The state of the roads

Fig. 7.6A (right): Steamer berthed at Tarbert Pier, looking west [*Cairt Phostail* series postcard: 2014]. Fig. 7.6B (above): The car loading berth at the Tarbert terminal in East Loch Tarbert. At the head of the loch can be seen the new buildings of the Harris Distillery Company [Photograph: Michael Cope].

in Harris and Barra can be assessed from some of Archie's photographs (Figs. 7.7 & 7.8).

For most people at the end of the 19th century the regular means of travel would have been by foot with pack ponies and creels used for carrying goods and materials (Figs. 7.9 & 7.10). The more affluent might have had access to a horse and two-wheeled cart (Fig. 7.11) or a four-wheeled trap and pair (Fig. 7.18A).

Roads and Fords

The major routes across the islands follow the earlier drove roads dating back at least to the 16th century. In *The Drove Roads of Scotland*[33] A. R. B. Haldane notes:

> One of the first to engage in the cattle trade between Uist, Skye and the mainland is believed to have been Donald MacDonald Third of Castle Camus, Skye, who at the end of the 16th and beginning of the 17th centuries established a regular trade in ponies and cattle.

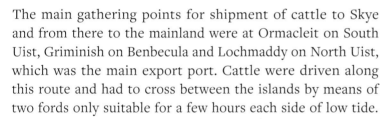

Fig 7.7A (left): Road from Rodel to Obbe (*An t-Ob*), Harris, looking north. The old Smithy is on the right [*Cairt Phostail* series postcard: 2037].

Fig 7.7B (above): The scene today – the Smithy survives in altered form as a private residence [Photograph: Michael Cope].

The main gathering points for shipment of cattle to Skye and from there to the mainland were at Ormacleit on South Uist, Griminish on Benbecula and Lochmaddy on North Uist, which was the main export port. Cattle were driven along this route and had to cross between the islands by means of two fords only suitable for a few hours each side of low tide.

Fig 7.8A (left): Road from Kentangval to Castlebay, Barra, looking south [*Cairt Phostail* series postcard: 2603].

Fig 7.8B (above): Today, with tarmac road, street lights and electricity transmission lines [Photograph: Michael Cope].

Fig. 7.9: Pack ponies carrying goods at Castlebay, Barra [*Cairt Phostail* series postcard: 2618A].

Fig. 7.10: *Each Chleibh* (pony with creel) [*Cairt Phostail* series postcard: 2611].

Fig. 7.11: Horse and cart at a Uist fair [Detail from original Archie Chisholm photograph: 1928; image © NMS].

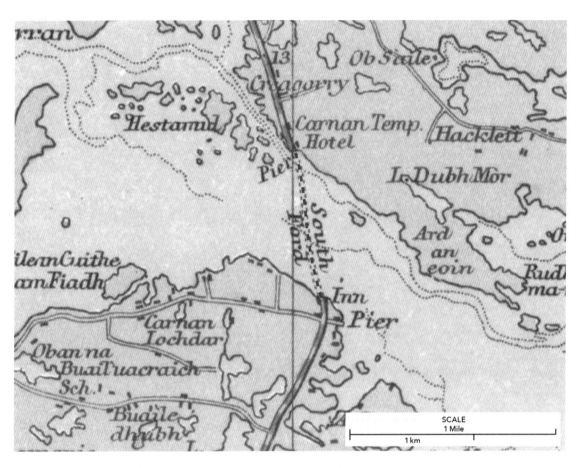

These were the South Ford between Carnan, South Uist and Creagorry, Benbecula (Figs. 7.12, 7.14 7.15 & 7.16) and the North Ford between Gramisdale, Benbecula and Carinish, North Uist (Figs. 7.13, 7.17, 7.18 & 7.19). According to Haldane the last droves of island cattle across Skye were made about 1906.

The fords remained the only means of land transportation between the islands until 1942 when the South Ford Bridge was built (replaced by a causeway opened in 1982). Before the North Ford causeway was opened in 1960 the crossing was always difficult and dangerous, as described on the

Fig. 7.12 (above): Route of the South Ford as shown on the Bartholomew's half-inch map Sheet 18, published 1904; reproduced by permission of the NLS.

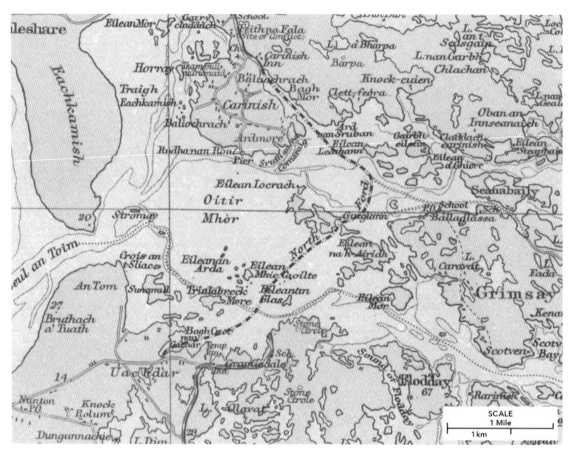

Fig. 7.13 (above): Route of the North Ford as shown on the Bartholomew's half-inch map Sheet 18, published 1904; reproduced by permission of the NLS.

Comhairle nan Eilean Siar website:[34]

The North Ford which the causeway replaced could only be crossed when the tide was out with the help of expert guides, who were often faced with tracing new routes after winter storms moved the sandbanks. At high tide a boat plied between Carinish and Gramisdale. The ford, marked by a series of cairns, was practicable on foot in fine weather and during spring tides – but it was four miles long and open for only one hour either side of low tide.

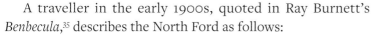

Fig. 7.14A (left): South Ford and Benbecula from Carnan [*Cairt Phostail* series postcard: 2401].
Fig. 7.14B (above): Entrance to the South Ford at Carnan today. On the right is the new causeway built in 1982 (Photograph: Michael Cope).

Fig. 7.15A (left): Entrance to the South Ford at Creagorry, Benbecula [*Cairt Phostail* series postcard: 2308; scan courtesy of Norman Hudson].
Fig. 7.15B (above): Entrance to the South Ford at Creagorry today. In the background is the new causeway built in 1982 – the old beacon gradually disintegrated from the action of weather and tides to disappear a decade or so later [Photograph: Michael Cope].

A traveller in the early 1900s, quoted in Ray Burnett's *Benbecula*,[35] describes the North Ford as follows:

Before us lay miles of mud and water, interspersed with islets and black rock and dark tangles of seaweed clinging to them. His guide told him that losing the path was dangerous. A yard or two to either side of it means that you are in quicksands

95

Fig. 7.16A (right): Creagorry Inn looking south towards the entrance to the South Ford [*Cairt Phostail* series postcard: 2307].

Fig. 7.16B (above): The much modernised and extended Isle of Benbecula Hotel today [Photograph: Alastair Chisholm].

Fig. 7.17A (right): Entrance to the North Ford at Carinish, North Uist [*Cairt Phostail* series postcard: 2199; scan courtesy of Norman Hudson].

Fig. 7.17B (above): Entrance to the North Ford at Carinish looking towards Benbecula today [Photograph: Michael Cope].

which immediately swallow any man, horse, cart or trap that deviates from the path.

There were inns on either side of the South Ford at Carnan and Creagorry and the North Ford at Gramisdale and Carinish. Archie photographed those at Creagorry and Carinish.

The inn at Creagorry was converted from the ferryman's

Fig. 7.18A (left): End of North Ford and Carinish [*Cairt Phostail* series postcard: 2200].
Fig. 7.18B (above): End of the North Ford looking towards Carinish today [Photograph: Michael Cope].

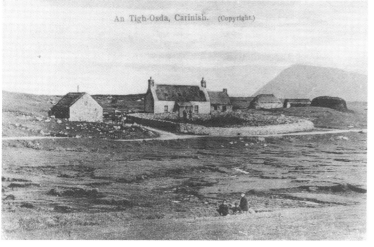

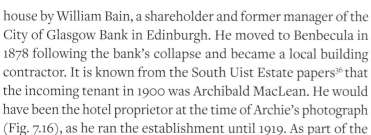

Fig. 7.19A (left): Carinish Inn (An Tigh-Osda) [*Cairt Phostail* series postcard: 2193; image © NMS].
Fig. 7.19B (above): Site of the former inn at Carinish today, now a centre belonging to the Free Church of Scotland [Photograph: Michael Cope].

house by William Bain, a shareholder and former manager of the City of Glasgow Bank in Edinburgh. He moved to Benbecula in 1878 following the bank's collapse and became a local building contractor. It is known from the South Uist Estate papers[36] that the incoming tenant in 1900 was Archibald MacLean. He would have been the hotel proprietor at the time of Archie's photograph (Fig. 7.16), as he ran the establishment until 1919. As part of the hotel's business it hired horses and traps to Carnan and Carinish for crossing the fords. It is now known as the Isle of Benbecula Hotel. The inn at Carinish, in Archie's time was known as An Tigh-Osda (Fig. 7.19). It was closed in November 2008 and has since been renovated and extended to provide a church, manse, meeting hall and café belonging to the Free Church of Scotland.

Sails and Wheels

As most villages were close to the coast the connection between these communities was more likely to be by sailing or rowing boat (Fig. 7.20). F. G. Rea provides us with some accounts[26] of travel by boat in the 1890s.

On the crossing from South Uist to Eriskay with Father Allan MacDonald he recalled:

> I watched Father Allan start the fire [of seaweed]... Father Allan gazed intently at this island [Eriskay] for a time and then left our perch to put more damp seaweed on the fire which gave off a denser smoke... This performance had been repeated several times, when, gazing across again, he sat down with an exclamation of satisfaction. Looking steadily across the sound, which was some two to three miles wide, I could see a column of smoke rising from a high point on the opposite shore. Our signal was answered! My companion said that the answering smoke signified that his signal had been seen and a boat would come for him.

The crossing itself in the hands of the ferryman and his son was not uneventful:

> There was a sudden Gaelic exclamation, down came the sail, and the boat slowed to a standstill. To my surprise, overboard went the old man and the boy, and they were standing in the water beside the boat and pushing – we were on a sandbank.

I looked round at Father Allan – he had taken off his boots and socks and was rolling up the legs of his trousers as far as he could. Telling me to remain where I was he was overboard in a minute pushing the boat with his shoulders like the others. With a gentle 'sweesh!' she slid into deep water as they all three clambered aboard.

Fig. 7.20 (left): Three men in a sailing boat, probably coast of North Uist [Original Archie Chisholm photograph reproduced from the lantern slide collection of Margaret Paterson: 1911].

Not all journeys by boat around the islands had such happy outcomes. The seas could be hazardous with unpredictable weather and currents affecting even short journeys.

F. G. Rea recounts an accident observed from the coast of Eriskay when out walking on another occasion with Father Allan:

I noticed a large boat in full sail about three miles away coming towards us from Barra. On my calling attention to it Father Allan said: 'That will be the fishing girls returning from the fisheries on the mainland: I know they are expected today.' … I happened to glance out again to where we had seen the boat. There was no sign of it. 'Where's the boat?' I called out. Not a boat was in sight. Father Allan said 'Something has gone wrong!' and we hurried off for help.

In an incredibly short time boats were launched and a search for the missing boat commenced… The boat and its occupants were never seen again. It was surmised that a sudden short unexpected squall of wind had struck and capsized her and she had sunk like a stone. I the better understood now the attitude of inimical fear of the sea that I had sensed at times among the people.

The most 'modern' transport photographed by Archie was the bicycle, with several enthusiasts photographed outside the Lochmaddy Courthouse in 1897 (Fig. 7.21). An anecdote about the first bicycle to be seen on South Uist is recounted by F. G. Rea:

As the object came nearer it dawned upon me that it was a man on a bicycle – a strange sight for our island! … it was MacQueen from the estate office… I asked him how long he had had it. 'Only a few days,' he said, 'but it is the first bicycle ever brought to the island.' … Then he began to laugh and told me that the women were afraid of it, for if they saw him with it they scurried into their houses and quickly shut the doors. But the men had made a great tumult about it and had been to the factor complaining that it frightened the horses and cattle, and they wanted the bicycle banished from the island. The factor took the part of his clerk and told them that the animals would soon get used to it. As the estate agent for the whole of the estate in the Outer Hebrides the factor had great authority; so MacQueen kept his bicycle.

Motor transport was not generally known in the Outer Isles until after WW1, but in the early 1900s a few private cars were introduced by estate owners and wealthy professionals. An article in the *Highland News* of 26th August 1899 reported:

Fig. 7.21: Three men with bicycles and a child in an early pushchair in Lochmaddy [Original Archie Chisholm photograph: 1121; image © NMS].

AN INNOVATION: the first motor car ever seen in Lewis was landed at Stornoway on Monday from the *Princess Ena* (Langlands). On its arrival, the horseless machine occupied by a few prominent citizens was driven several times through the principal streets and attracted no little attention. The motor was brought to Lewis by Mr W. K. Millar who had taken a lease of the Soval shootings.

We can find no similar reports for the appearance of the first motor transports in Harris, the Uists or Barra. The earliest firm record for the presence of a motor car in Harris is provided by Tony Scherr in *A History of Borve Lodge*.[37] He states that in 1911 the estate owner, the 8th Earl of Dunmore, extended the lodge and upgraded the outbuildings to include a double garage used to house a Darracq motor car. The first motor car on Berneray was as late as 1933 when Finlay Paterson introduced a Morgan three-wheeler to the island, first registered in Glasgow in 1923.[38]

Chapter 8

Post Offices, the Mail and the Telegraph

As described in the previous chapter the establishment of regular mail services to the Outer Isles grew from the packet sailing ships maintained by the estate owners to help manage their island interests. As the national postal service was extended in the 19th century, so post offices were maintained for public benefit and at public expense by the General Post Office (GPO) on the various islands. The history of the posts and the post offices of the islands has been comprehensively described by James A. Mackay in his booklets *Islands Postal History Series, Volumes 1, 2 & 3*.[28, 29, 30] His notes relating to the post offices that featured in Archie's photographs are particularly relevant to this chapter.

Post Offices on Harris

At the time Archie arrived in the Long Island the postal service in Harris was not well served by a system administered from Lewis with all external mail having to go through Stornoway irrespective of its destination. The prevailing situation was such that a letter from Obbe to Lochmaddy (ten miles in distance) took a route of 200 miles via Stornoway and the mainland and five days to be delivered! The overland mail from Tarbert to Stornoway was carried along a rough road across the high hills of the Forest of Harris by two messengers twice a week in summer and once a week in winter. The journey is described, not much improved, some years later in Ada Goodrich-Frecr's *Outer Isles*:[32]

> In places the high road makes some demands upon the fortitude of the nervous traveller, and the merciful one will certainly travel

Fig. 8.1A (right): The Lochmaddy post office [*Cairt Phostail* series postcard: 2117]. Fig. 8.1B (above): The scene today with the site functioning as a car park. The superficially similar building seen in the background was built after the original photograph was taken. [Photograph: Michael Cope]. Fig. 8.1C: Lochmaddy postmark from 1883, reproduced from Mackay, 1978.

some miles of the journey on his own feet, though the excellent horses sent for us from Tarbert are an equine pleasure...

The *Inverness Courier* reported on a public meeting held in Tarbert on 24th November 1885 to consider the postal, passenger and traffic communications between Harris and the mainland. At this the Earl of Dunmore (the owner of Harris and Chairman of the meeting) said 'there was no doubt that the present means of communication was very defective, circuitous and absurdly disjointed' – and by implication clearly not in the interests of the management of his estate. One of the resolutions passed at the meeting requested that a regular steamer service for the mail should be established connecting Harris to North Uist and Skye. Another resolution was passed to cooperate with North Uist to achieve the same results. A petition was to be drawn up by the Earl and forwarded to the Postmaster General.

Unfortunately Archie left no photographic images of the Harris post offices as he did for those on the islands further south, although the rooftop of the Tarbert post and telegraph office can be seen nestling below the road wall in his picture of the town from the southern approach road (see Fig. 9.1). The

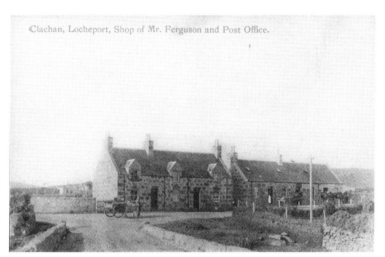

Clachan, Locheport, Shop of Mr. Ferguson and Post Office.

Fig. 8.2A (left): Clachan (Locheport) post office [*Cairt Phostail* series postcard: 2187; scan courtesy of Norman Hudson].
Fig. 8.2B (above): The scene today with the old post office rebuilt as the new Clachan Stores in 1984–1985; it closed as a post office in 2015. [Photograph: Michael Cope].
Fig. 8.2C: Clachan-Locheport postmark from 1891, reproduced from Mackay, 1978.

building is now the shop of the Harris Tweed Isle of Harris company.

Post Offices on North Uist

A post office was first established on North Uist in 1802 at Carinish, about a mile from the landing place of the Dunvegan to Claddach Carinish sailing packet. In 1828 Lord MacDonald's factor Duncan Shaw was appointed Postmaster, and as he lived in Lochmaddy the post office moved there for his convenience. As a result the packet service then sailed from Dunvegan to Lochmaddy and remained in service until 1886. From Lochmaddy the mail was distributed by a series of 'runners' who carried the mail by foot to other parts of the island.

In 1878 a new post office was built at Lochmaddy and the link to Carinish was upgraded from a 'runner' to a 'horse post'. It was this building that Archie photographed for one of his postcards (Fig. 8.1). Eventually this office became too small for the volume of mail passing through and another new office was built in 1905. The previous office, shown on the postcard, became the Stag

Newton Ferry. (Copyright.)

Fig. 8.3A (right): Newton Ferry post office [*Cairt Phostail* series postcard: 2103].

Fig. 8.3B (above): Site of former Newton Ferry post office, some of the original building stones remain behind the farm store [Photograph: Michael Cope].

Fig. 8.3C: Newton Ferry postmark from 1886, reproduced from Mackay, 1978.

Lodge Guest House which continued in that function until it was destroyed by fire in 2001. The site of the building is now a car park for the Hamersay House Hotel.

Also in 1878 two new sub-post offices were opened in North Uist: one at Clachan (later becoming Locheport in 1881; Fig. 8.2), and another at Newton Ferry near the old Sound of Harris ferry landing at Port nan Long (Fig. 8.3). The former was reconstructed as the Clachan Stores in 1984–1985, but the latter has been demolished.

According to accounts in Mackay, Sir John Campbell-Orde had several disputes with the Lochmaddy postmasters of the day indicating his feuds with public officials were not confined to the Procurator Fiscal. In 1883 the Postmaster Mr Macaskill was dismissed by Sir John for drunkenness, but reinstated on appeal the following year. He was subsequently evicted from his house in May 1885 and, having found himself with no abode, lost his job with the GPO.

In 1885, now living at Claddach-Kirkibost, Mr Macaskill reappears in the story of the North Uist posts as a proponent of the status quo when changes to the mail delivery system from the mainland were proposed by the GPO. Mail came directly to Lochmaddy by sailing packet from Dunvegan in Skye with a scheduled daily service. The GPO wished to discontinue the packet and replace the delivery across the Minch with a three times weekly steamship service from Oban. To run the service the GPO had agreed to pay the Highland Fisheries Company an annual subsidy of £2,000; at that time the Skye packet was estimated to cost only about £500 a year.

A vigorous local campaign against the changes was led by the local Free Church minister Mr Mackinnon, supported by Mr Macaskill. Public meetings were held in Lochmaddy, Sollas and Paible and resolutions passed requesting the postal authorities to rethink their decision. A petition was also organised to show the strength of public opinion on the matter. An animated correspondence took place in the pages of the *Inverness Courier* from October 1885 to January 1886 involving Mackinnon and Macaskill, among others, on one side and Archie and Sheriff-Substitute James Webster on the other.

The status quo argument stressed the daily nature of the existing packet service, and included assertions of a lack of transparency in the GPO's dealings with the Highland Fisheries Company and the seeming favourable nature of the arrangements to the company and the South Uist and Barra fisheries, all to the detriment of the North Uist community. Archie and Webster argued that the suggestion of impropriety on behalf of the GPO was unfounded and that perhaps the public meetings had been manipulated to favour the status quo, both matters of fairness from their legal perspective.

Archie also challenged the reliability of the so called 'daily' service. He noted that the ship frequently could not sail due to bad weather or calm weather and so he quite often received mail only once a week. But, crucially, Archie and Webster argued that Harris, part of their jurisdiction, was completely cut off from the rest of insular Inverness-shire and that any changes to the mail system should involve Harris.

Out of all of this surfaced a proposal backed by Archie, Webster and the Earl of Dunmore (the owner of Harris) that a new steamship service should be established, but that this should be a new triangular route Dunvegan-Lochmaddy-Obbe-Tarbert-Dunvegan, so connecting the currently disjointed parts of Inverness-shire.

In spite of all the controversy the GPO pushed ahead with its plans for the Oban steamer service, but it was reported in the *Edinburgh Evening News* on 13th January 1886 that:

> One or two companies were started and one or two more were projected on the faith of the mail steamer beginning on the 1st of January, but all these hopes and prospects of livelier times are fast vanishing as no steamer has appeared, but on the contrary the old sailing packets have been re-engaged.

Eventually the GPO announced that the new Oban steamship route would commence on 1st March 1886, but that the service would terminate at Castlebay via Lochboisdale; a year later it was finally extended to Lochmaddy.

As a result of the lobbying of Archie, Webster and the Earl of Dunmore a new mail connection between North Uist, Harris and Skye was eventually established in the summer of 1886 with a contract awarded to David MacBrayne Ltd to deploy its new steamer *Staffa* on the route. This was the achievement relating to mail services mentioned by Thomas Wilson at Archie's presentation on leaving Lochmaddy in 1913 (see Chapter 2). The sailing packet, the cutter *Dream*, was withdrawn and, after overhaul in Greenock in May 1887, was offered for sale by an advertisement in the *Inverness Courier* on 29th June 1888. The subsequent history of the vessel is not known.

Post Offices on Benbecula and South Uist

The first post office on Benbecula dates from the 1840s when a receiving house was established at Nunton along the 'runner' route between Lochmaddy, North Uist and Kilbride, South Uist using the North and South Fords. A few decades later, in response to the south of the island becoming increasingly prosperous due to tourism and the volume of mail thus increasing, a new post office was opened at Creagorry in 1878. James Mackay states that the office was the former police station opposite the inn, but inspection of the Ordnance Survey map of 1903 shows the post office clearly marked around 1km further north at the Balivanich road junction. The exact location of the photograph taken by Archie (Fig. 8.4) may never be known, but the small amount of landscape detail in the background strongly suggests the latter roadside location.

South Uist had very rudimentary postal services in the early 19th century, being served by 'runners' from Carinish or Lochmaddy via the two fords. The earliest post office was established as a receiving house at Kilbride in the south of the island in 1839

Fig. 8.4A (left): The post office at Creagorry [*Cairt Phostail* series postcard: 2305].

Fig. 8.4B (below): Probable site of old Creagorry post office at the Balivanich junction on the A865 road [Photograph: Michael Cope].

Fig. 8.4C: Creagorry postmark from 1880, reproduced from Mackay, 1978.

Fig. 8.5A (right): The post office at Howmore [*Cairt Phostail* series postcard: 2404].
Fig. 8.5B (above): Site of the old post office at Howmore [Photograph: Michael Cope].
Fig. 8.5C: Howmore postmark from 1908, reproduced from Mackay, 1978.

and in 1843 another was established at Howmore, in the centre of the island. Eventually Howmore was linked with Creagorry by a horse post in 1882 (Fig. 8.6) with the letter carrier paid 16 shillings (£0.80) per week plus 4 shillings (£0.20) per week for upkeep of the horse – a handsome salary for the time. In spite of the growth of the horse posts new foot post services were being established on South Uist until as late as 1907. The building at Howmore photographed by Archie (Fig. 8.5) has been demolished and replaced by a modern bungalow.

Fig. 8.6: Horse post on the North Ford [*Cairt Phostail* series postcard: 2201; scan courtesy of Norman Hudson].

Post Offices on Eriskay and Barra

The Eriskay sub-post office was opened in November 1885. Ada Goodrich-Freer[32] describes a visit she made to the office in 1894:

> The post-office is an important centre of business. The post-master can write English, and one constantly finds him occupied with secretarial work, and that not only of a private nature, the communication with distant friends, but also as it sounds, over £500 a year goes out from Eriskay – with a population of about 500 – for goods sent by parcel post.

Marjory Kennedy-Fraser in her autobiography *A Life In Song*[39] recalls her later visit to the post office in 1905:

> The post office was a little thatched cottage which, unlike the majority of the old 'black houses', could boast a chimney and a triple partition. Here I soon made the acquaintance of the courteous, well-informed, postal official, Dougall MacMillan, and his beautiful, dignified old sister, Mairi Mhor. Their little, clean, sanded kitchen, with its tiny, home-made, dresser, adorned with painted bowls and jugs, its two wooden benches along the wall, with accommodation below for peats, its barrel of flour topped with baking board (serving as a kitchen table), and its bag of oatmeal by the fire, was the recognised rendezvous of the island.

Unfortunately Archie did not photograph Dougall MacMillan or his sister, but his photograph of the office itself perfectly fits with Kennedy-Fraser's description (Fig. 8.7). Dougall MacMillan remained as postmaster until 1945, but the cottage is long since demolished and the replacement building described by James Mackay was also demolished in 2017.

A post office was first established on Barra at Eoligarry in 1855, following successful lobbying of the GPO by the island's owner, Colonel Gordon. Later a sub-post office was opened in Pier

Fig. 8.7A (right): The post office at Eriskay [*Cairt Phostail* series postcard: 2502].
Fig. 8.7B (above): Site of the old post office at Eriskay [Photograph: Michael Cope].
Fig. 8.7C: Eriskay postmark from 1902 reproduced from Mackay, 1978.

Road in Castlebay in 1875. Unfortunately in Archie's photograph looking down Pier Road the post office is obscured by another building, since demolished to widen the road (see Fig. 9.17A). Today, the original building still functions as a post office and also as Macroon's Tea Room.

Use of the *Cairt Phostail* Series Picture Postcards

Several examples of postally used cards in our collection suggest that Archie's postcards were widely used by visitors to the islands. Most are dated during Archie's Lochmaddy years, with the earliest known postmark being Lochmaddy, December 1904. Our first records from South Uist are 1906 from Lochboisdale, from Harris in 1907 and posted on the mainland at Beauly in 1905. The latest known use of a card was in 1961, posted at Forres, Morayshire. Some postmarked examples are shown in Figs. 8.8–8.10. Michael Gardner in his history of Finsbay Lodge on Harris notes:

> The Hebridean Sporting Association's accounts show that the Lodge had a considerable stock of postcards (worth £8 3s 0d in 1916), presumably emanating from Chisholm's camera.

CAIRT PHOSTAIL.

CUIR AN SEOLADH AIR AN TAOBH SEO

Angus A. Macpherson Esq.
The Prescott National Bank.
Prescott,
Arizona.

Fig. 8.8: *Cairt Phostail* posted at Beauly, 11th September 1905.

Fig. 8.9: *Cairt Phostail* posted at Lochboisdale Pier 30th May 1906.

Fig. 8.10: *Cairt Phostail* posted at Harris, 16th September 1907 and received at Portree later the same day.

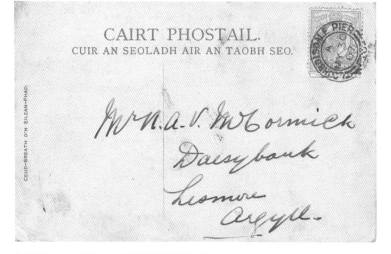

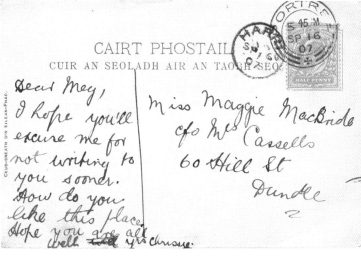

So here at least is one record of a commercial outlet for the postcards. It is assumed that the hotels and general stores throughout the islands were also stockists for the cards.

The Telegraph

The GPO oversaw the establishment of the telegraph system throughout the Hebrides. This would have been not long in existence when Archie first came to Lochmaddy.

Alison Taubman in her article 'Electric Telegraph to e-Scotland: Networking remote and rural communities'[40] explains that the telegraph cable from Stornoway to the mainland was completed on 28th June 1872 as part of the Highland and Islands scheme 1870-1872 to extend the national telegraph network. Another cable from Lochmaddy on North Uist to Rodel on Harris was laid by 5th July 1872; this cost £1,042 to lay across the Sound of Harris – to generate only £73 of revenue at Lochmaddy! The link from Stornoway to Tarbert and Rodel was completed by overland wires the same year. By 1883 the telegraph system had been extended to Barra.

In all the roadside views taken by Archie the telegraph poles and wires are clearly visible (Figs. 4.17, 7.11 & 7.21). The post offices also acted as telegraph offices with the appropriate signage evident in Figs. 8.3, 8.4 & 8.7.

There was also a radio transmitting station at Lochboisdale, located next to the Lochboisdale Hotel and termed the 'Marconi Pole' by Archie (Fig. 8.11). This was not part of the domestic telegraph network, but used to communicate by Morse code to the Atlantic fleet based at Rosyth; it was operated by the GPO on behalf of the Admiralty.

C. Mackay responding to the posting of this picture (Fig. 8.11A) on the *Tasglann nan Eilean Siar* blogsite comments in 2013:[41]

Lochboisdale, "Marconi" pole. (Copyright.)

Fig. 8.11A (left): The 'Marconi Pole' at Lochboisdale [*Cairt Phostail* series postcard: 2412; scan courtesy of Norman Hudson].

Fig. 8.11B (below): Site of the former telegraph mast at Lochboisdale, now the local cattle market [Photograph: Michael Cope].

My grandfather was a telegraph linesman with the Post Office Telephones. Though he was born in Eilean Shona we are a Uist family. We never knew of the Marconi Station at Lochboisdale till now. Usually he worked in Glasgow but this would explain why he moved back to Uist with the family in 1907–8 (probably posted back).

This account fits perfectly with the operation of the antenna in Archie's time at Lochmaddy. After that, from January 1913 to August 1914, the mast was used for communication with St Kilda. Its subsequent use is not fully known. A wireless telegraph station as a feature is marked on Ordnance Survey maps published in 1947, but not recorded when the area was resurveyed in 1956. The site of the mast is now occupied by the local cattle market.

Chapter 9

The Main Settlements

Population

At the 1881 official census of Scotland the Inverness-shire part
of the Outer Isles had a total population of 17,521, living in 3,465
separate families. According to the definitions at the time there
were no designated towns or villages, as all of the population
was classified as living in rural areas (enumeration districts
with less than 300 people) and most of those would have lived
in crofting townships. At the last census before Archie left the
Long Island the situation had not much changed with 17,129
people in 3,769 families. Population figures[42] for the various
islands during these years were:

ISLAND	1881	1891	1901	1911
Harris	4,814	5,024	5,271	5,449
North Uist	4,264	4,187	3,891	3,677
South Uist	6,078	5,821	5,516	5,383
Barra	2,365	2,161	2,545	2,620
Total	17,521	17,193	17,223	17,129

On each island the main hubs of trade and commerce were
well established when Archie arrived – Tarbert, Lochmaddy,
Lochboisdale and Castlebay, places with harbours, steamer
terminals, hotels, general stores, post offices and associated

activity. Archie provided a good turn of the century record of these main settlements in a number of his topographic photographs – the majority were taken in Lochmaddy where he lived and worked, but the other main settlements are also represented. They are shown here north to south.

Fig. 9.1A: Tarbert looking west from the southeast approach [*Cairt Phostail* series postcard: 2015].

Tarbert, Harris [*An Tairbeart, Na Hearadh*]

Tarbert is the main settlement on Harris and derives its name from the Norse word for a point where boats could be pulled across – in this case between the East and West lochs. This activity was recorded in 1786 by John Knox, referring to fishermen in pursuit of herring shoals. He suggested building a canal between the two lochs or constructing a good road to aid the fishermen in their task. Lord Leverhulme revived the idea of a canal in the early 20th century, but his plans were never put into effect.[43]

In the early 19th century Tarbert was little more than a hamlet, but it developed into a more substantive village in the second half of the century with a population of 535 by 1901 (Fig. 9.1). Along with the village's growth the Tarbert Hotel was built in 1865 by the 7th Earl of Dunmore. At the time he owned the North

Harris Estate and built the hotel as a 'sporting retreat' for anglers (Fig. 9.2); it was renamed the Harris Hotel in 1903. We know that Archie made photographic tours of Harris sometime in 1903 and in May–June 1904, but it seems he never stayed at the hotel on those trips. Tarbert also became an important steamer terminal at this time (see Chapter 7, Figs. 7.4–7.6 for photographs of the pier in East Loch Tarbert).

Fig. 9.1B: Tarbert today from the footpath above the A859 road [Photograph: Michel Cope].

The Hotel, Tarbert, Harris, Scotland. (Copyright.)

Fig. 9.2A (left): The Tarbert Hotel, Harris [*Cairt Phostail* series postcard: 2009].
Fig. 9.2B (above): View of the hotel today (now the Harris Hotel) showing several new extensions [Photograph: Michael Cope].

Lochmaddy, North Uist [*Loch nam Madadh, Uibhist a Tuath*]

The original name of the area where Lochmaddy developed was Cearsabhagh or Kersivay, probably derived from Norse as a description of the complex shape of the bay. By the 1600s *Loch nam Madadh* was the Gaelic name in use – a reference to the rocks in the entrance to the loch being shaped like the heads of dogs or wolves (*madadh*). In 1703 there was a quay at Lochmaddy,

Fig. 9.3A (right): The Old Courthouse at Lochmaddy [*Cairt Phostail* series postcard: 2122].
Fig. 9.3B (above): The Old Courthouse today – now a private residence [Photograph: Alastair Chisholm].

Fig. 9.4A (right): County Buildings and New Courthouse in Lochmaddy [*Cairt Phostail* series postcard: 2119].
Fig. 9.4B (above): The County Buildings today, still used as a Sheriff Court [Photograph: Alastair Chisholm].

and by 1802 a fishing village had developed to take advantage of the plentiful herring in nearby waters.[44] Lochmaddy took on the role as the administrative centre for Inverness-shire on the Long Island with the establishment of the office of Sheriff-Substitute and the building of a Sheriff Court. The original Courthouse (Fig. 9.3) dates from 1827, serving latterly as a prison from 1875 until 1891.

The new Sheriff Court opened in 1875 (Fig. 9.4), and this

Fig. 9.5A (left): Sponish House, residence of the Sheriff-Substitute [*Cairt Phostail* series postcard: 2110; scan courtesy of Norman Hudson].
Fig. 9.5B (below): Sponish House today, currently being converted into residential apartments [Photograph: Michael Cope].

Fig. 9.6A (left): The Lochmaddy Hotel, (D. Macfadyen, Proprietor) [*Cairt Phostail* series postcard: 2161].
Fig. 9.6B (above): The hotel today, considerably extended. The road in front has also been rebuilt to allow access to the ferry terminal [Photograph: Alastair Chisholm].

Lochmaddy from Market stance. (Copyright.)

Fig. 9.7A (right): Lochmaddy, looking northeast from the Market Stance [*Cairt Phostail* series postcard: 2128].
Fig. 9.7B (above): Lochmaddy today viewed from above the A865 road [Photograph: Michael Cope].

Sean Laimhrig agus Tigh-na-Cuirte etc. Loch-na-madaidh. (Copyright)

Fig. 9.8A (right): Lochmaddy, looking west from Oronsay towards the old jetty. Maclean's Mansion is prominent in the centre and the New Courthouse is on the right [*Cairt Phostail* series postcard: 2125].
Fig. 9.8B (above): Lochmaddy today with the derelict Maclean's Mansion prominent on the skyline [Photograph: Michael Cope].

would be the place where Archie subsequently worked. The Sheriff-Substitute originally occupied Sponish House designed and built for Lord MacDonald by James Gillespie Graham in 1803 (Fig. 9.5); more recently it has been restored as residential apartments.

Further growth in the early decades of the steamer traffic

Fig.9.9A (left): Lochmaddy School [*Cairt Phostail* series postcard: 2126].
Fig.9.9B (above): Lochmaddy School as it appeared in 2007 [Photograph: Alastair Chisholm].

saw leisure visitors coming for the fishing or shooting. The Lochmaddy Hotel (Fig. 9.6), built in 1864, was expanded in 1884 to cater for this new trade and at one time the hotel owned 29 boats on its various fishing lochs. The former Sheriff's residence at Sponish House also became used as a sporting lodge in the late 19th century.

By 1901 the official population of Lochmaddy was 247 and Archie's photographs show the substantial buildings of the village at the century's turn in several panoramas. Fig. 9.7 shows the view from the Market Stance above the Pier Road with the New Courthouse on the left, Ostrom House in the centre and The Bank House on the right. The prominent building in the centre of Fig. 9.8 is Lee View, also known as Maclean's Mansion (*Taigh Mòr Chlann Mhic Eachainn*), which was built c.1800 by John Maclean a merchant from Boreray as his 'townhouse'. According to the Canmore record[45] it served as a general store and multiple dwelling until 1950 when it became a Masonic lodge. It is now in a state of disrepair, on the buildings at risk register.

Lochmaddy School (Fig. 9.9) was opened in 1877, following the

Fig. 9.10A (right): Lochboisdale looking southeast towards the pier [*Cairt Phostail* series postcard: 2410].

Fig. 9.10B (above): The scene today with the car ferry loading terminal at the redeveloped pier [Photograph: Alastair Chisholm].

Fig. 9.11A (right): Lochboisdale looking northwest. The building centre-field is the Commercial Bank of Scotland and the building on the left is the Free Church of Scotland [*Cairt Phostail* series postcard: 2409].

Fig. 9.11B (above): The scene today; both the bank and church buildings have the same uses [Photograph: Alastair Chisholm].

requirement of the Education Act of 1872 which made education compulsory in Scotland, publicly financed and directed by elected School Boards. Archie's interest in this building as a subject for a photograph was probably influenced by his being a member of the North Uist School Board at that time. The school closed in 2016 following the opening of a new North Uist primary school at Paible.

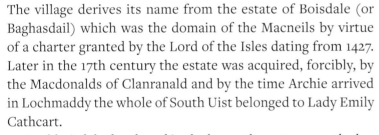

Lochboisdale, South Uist [*Loch Baghasdail, Uibhist a Deas*]

Fig. 9.12A (left): The Lochboisdale Hotel, Simon Mackenzie, Proprietor [*Cairt Phostail* series postcard: 2411; scan courtesy of Norman Hudson].
Fig. 9.12B (above): The hotel today with its new extensions [Photograph: Alastair Chisholm].

The village derives its name from the estate of Boisdale (or Baghasdail) which was the domain of the Macneils by virtue of a charter granted by the Lord of the Isles dating from 1427. Later in the 17th century the estate was acquired, forcibly, by the Macdonalds of Clanranald and by the time Archie arrived in Lochmaddy the whole of South Uist belonged to Lady Emily Cathcart.

Lochboisdale developed in the late 19th century mostly due to the herring fishing boom, aided by the good natural harbour provided by the sea loch. This led to construction of a steamer pier in 1880 and the opening of the Lochboisdale Hotel in 1882 (Figs. 9.10–9.12) to cater for the steamer trade. *The Ordnance Gazetteer of Scotland* (1882–1884)[46] describes Lochboisdale as follows:

> The hamlet lies near the head of the sea-loch, and has a post office under Lochmaddy, with money order and savings' bank departments. The loch... has a very indented outline and

numerous islets; is one of the best, safest, and largest harbours in the kingdom; and affords shelter to vessels in the Baltic trade under stress of weather.

Castlebay, Barra [*Bàgh a' Chaisteal, Barraigh*]

Castlebay takes its name from the medieval Kisimul Castle (*Caisteal Chiosmuil*) which sits on a rocky islet in a bay on

Fig. 9.13A (right): Castlebay Harbour, busy with fishing boats [*Cairt Phostail* series postcard: 2606].
Fig. 9.13B (below): Castlebay today with a quite deserted harbour [Photograph: Michael Cope].

Fig. 9.14A (right): Castlebay steamer jetty seen from Castlebay Hotel. [Original Archie Chisholm photograph: 1607; reproduced from illustration in W. C. Mackenzie's *History of the Outer Hebrides*]
Fig. 9.14B (above): The jetty today – with the car ferry loading terminal [Photograph: Michael Cope].

Castlebay. (Copyright.)

Fig. 9.15A (left): Kisimul Castle seen from Pier Road looking south [*Cairt Phostail* series postcard: 2612].
Fig. 9.15B (above): The view looking down Pier Road today – cars have replaced ponies [Photograph: Michael Cope].

the south coast of Barra. The age of the earliest surviving structures date from the early 15th century – Barra was granted to the Clan Macneil by the Lord of the Isles in 1427 – but from archaeological evidence occupation of the site itself may date back to the Bronze Age or Neolithic times.[47] The castle fell into disrepair and was left derelict for much of the 18th and 19th centuries. A restoration programme begun in 1937 by the Clan Chief Robert Macneil, an American architect, was completed in 1970. The castle is now in the care of Historic Environment Scotland.

In 1869 Castlebay was developed as a herring fishery port by James Methuen and by the time Archie visited in the 1890s it had become a thriving village with around 400 small fishing boats based there (Figs. 9.13–9.15). There was also the development of a successful associated herring curing and preserving industry.

Two churches were built in Castlebay, both overlooking the harbour: one by the Catholic Church in 1888, and one by the Church of Scotland in 1892 – both during Archie's time on the islands. The Catholic Church of Our Lady Star of the Sea (Fig. 10.5; and see Chapter 10 for more detail) survives in use, but the Church of Scotland has closed, being unable to find a viable congregation in this strongly Catholic area; it is now on the buildings at risk register.

The Castlebay Hotel had opened in the 1860s and Archie probably stayed there on his visits as several of his photographs were taken from the hotel terrace, although we do not have a photograph of the hotel itself. Unfortunately the guest records for this time have been lost. The hotel bar today has reproductions of many of Archie's photographs on its walls.

Chapter 10

Churches

The Church in Scotland

The large number of antiquities known as *Teampulls* surviving across the Outer Hebrides attests to the presence of many early Christian communities in medieval times (see Chapter 5). These communities eventually became the formalised Catholic Church through the first half of the second millennium. Scotland's Reformation in 1590 led to a complicated Protestant divergence, accompanied by multiple schisms and reunifications, into eight separately recognised churches today; the Catholic Church by contrast has continued quite unaffected by these doctrinal disputes.

In Archie's time the picture in the Long Island was just as diverse as today with a strong regional differentiation from a dominantly Catholic Barra in the south to a Free Church-dominated Lewis in the north. For all the denominations the period 1880–1900 was also a time of increased church construction, with many of the buildings of that era surviving in use today. Several of these buildings became the subject of Archie's photographs. Being a Catholic, his attention was mainly towards the Catholic churches. There are five photographed church buildings, all represented on *Cairt Phostail* postcards, shown here north to south.

Balranald (North Uist Parish) Church

Originally known as the North Uist Parish Church, this church is maintained by the Church of Scotland in its present-day parish of Kilmuir and Paible, close to the village of Balranald (Fig. 10.1).[48] It

Parish Church of North Uist. (Copyright.)

Fig. 10.1A (right): North Uist Parish Church, Balranald [*Cairt Phostail* series postcard: 2178].
Fig. 10.1B (above): North Uist Parish (now Kilmuir) Church today [Photograph: Alastair Chisholm].

was constructed to a gothic design by Alexander Sharp in 1892–1894. It displays a two-stage tower with its battlemented parapet enclosing a slated pyramidal spire; inside there is a wealth of pitch-pine. It is one of the few remaining churches where, during the morning Gaelic service, one can still participate in the presenting of Gaelic psalms.

St Mary's Church, Benbecula

This Catholic church was constructed in 1884 (Fig. 10.2). For its 125th anniversary in 2009 the parish priest Father Ross Crichton explained to the *Stornoway Gazette:*[49]

> The parish itself has seen many changes over its 125 year history most notably the addition of the North Ford causeway which certainly makes the journey to the church much easier. Since then, the island has been served by a succession of priests, resident on Benbecula. Prior to this, the parish was served by priests from South Uist who had to cross the ford to reach the island – no easy task in the pre-causeway days!

Fig. 10.2A (left): St Mary's Church, Benbecula [*Cairt Phostail* series postcard: 2302; cropped image reproduced from B. Charnley: *The Western Isles: A Postcard Tour*, Vol. 1]. Fig. 10.2B (above): St Mary's Church today [Photograph: Alastair Chisholm].

He also noted that the island of Benbecula looks back to a very long history of Christian activity:

> Benbecula's earliest Christian site is situated near Balivanich and named after St Columba [*Teampull Chalumchille*, Fig. 5.8]... Celtic monks and nuns were present on the island in the middle ages. The very origins of names 'Balivanich' (*Baile a'Mhanaich* – i.e. Monkton) and 'Nunton' (*Baile na Cailleach*) bear witness to their presence. The current Church carries the name of the ruined medieval chapel in Nunton, St Mary's.

St Peter's Church, Daliburgh, South Uist

This Catholic church was built in 1868, originally incorporating the priest's house under the same roof (Fig. 10.3). Its stone font comes from the medieval chapel of St Coineach, which stood at Auratot near Lochboisdale. According to the Canmore record,[50] the attached brick-built presbytery was added in 1907. In the picture it appears newly built and so the photograph was probably taken not long after its construction. The associated

Fig. 10.3A (right): St Peter's Church, South Uist (the caption: *Eaglais Chatiliceach 'us Tigh an t-Sagairt, Dhalibrog*, translates as: Catholic Church and Presbytery, Dalabrog) [*Cairt Phostail* series postcard: 2406; scan courtesy of Norman Hudson]. Fig. 10.3B (above): St Peter's Church today [Photograph: Alastair Chisholm].

school dates from 1876, one of a clutch of island schools based on Alexander Ross's standard design.

St Michael's Church, Eriskay

St Michael's of the Sea is a Catholic church constructed in 1899–1903 (Fig. 10.4).[51] It was built by the islanders themselves using local stone, timber salvaged from wrecks and a cement mortar of burnt shells and sand under the guidance of the first incumbent priest Father Allan MacDonald;[52] funds for additional materials were raised locally from the proceeds of fishing, and from abroad. It replaced a more humble structure dating from 1852. The nearby presbytery dates from 1891.

Father Allan MacDonald was a good friend of Frederick Rea and is frequently referred to in *A School in South Uist*.[26] He is known for rowing a boat from Kilbride on South Uist to Eriskay once a week while tending to his 'flock' on the island. Father Allan is the priest seen on the path in front of the church in Archie's

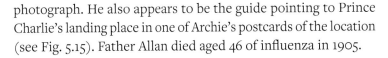

Fig. 10.4A (left): St Michael's Church, Eriskay (the caption: *An t-Urramach Maighstir Ailean 'us am Pobull an deidh n' aifrionn, an Eriskay,* translates as: The Reverend Father Allan and the people after his service on Eriskay) [*Cairt Phostail* series postcard: 2501; scan courtesy of Norman Hudson].

Fig. 10.4B (above): St Michael's Church today [Photograph: Michael Cope].

photograph. He also appears to be the guide pointing to Prince Charlie's landing place in one of Archie's postcards of the location (see Fig. 5.15). Father Allan died aged 46 of influenza in 1905.

Church of Our Lady, Star of the Sea, Castlebay, Barra

Writing on the Barra Catholic Church website,[53] Mary Ceit MacKinnon provides a brief history of the church of Our Lady, Star of the Sea:

> With the growing population of Castlebay it had become increasingly apparent that a new church was required, but it was difficult to obtain the necessary funding as the majority of people were poor with little money to spare. However in 1886 the Castlebay merchant, Neil MacNeil, died and he bequeathed the sum of eight hundred pounds for the purposes of obtaining a suitable piece of ground and on it building a church. Roderick Campbell offered a part of his croft for this purpose and this

Fig. 10.5A: The Catholic Church of Our Lady Star of the Sea – this photograph taken before demolition of the adjacent blackhouse and addition of a retaining wall and approach road; compare with Fig. 10.5B [*Cairt Phostail* series postcard: 2609].

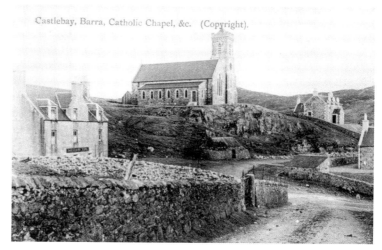

Castlebay, Barra, Catholic Chapel, &c. (Copyright).

was readily accepted. Following this John Campbell suggested that a small quarry be opened on his croft as the rock there was granite and was suitable for building purposes. Such a generous offer could not be refused. The architect G. Woulfe Brennan was commissioned to design the new building. The contractors chosen were MacDougall and MacColl of Oban.

In January 1891 a bell and clock were added to the church tower – paid for by money collected locally. In March 1892 work was begun on building the Chapel House so that the priest's residence could be at Castlebay rather than at Craigston.

The church opened on Christmas Eve 1888 when people from all around the islands gathered for Midnight Mass. The newly finished church could seat 800 people and on that occasion it was filled to capacity. The new parish priest was Canon James Chisholm and the sermon was preached by the famous Father Allan MacDonald of Eriskay.

James Chisholm was a distant relation of Archie through the Lietry branch of the family – sharing a great-great-grandfather in Colin Chisholm by separate marriages. It is possible through this family connection that Archie attended the opening of the church,

Fig. 10.5B: Church of Our Lady Star of the Sea photographed after construction of the approach road, demolition of the adjacent blackhouses and building of a boundary wall. *Cairt Phostail* series postcard: 2610].

Fig. 10.5C: The view of the church today, Alastair Chisholm in the foreground [Photograph: Colin Chisholm].

but we have no confirmation of this. The Chisholms originally came from Strathglass in Inverness-shire which was one of the residual enclaves of the Catholic tradition in the Highlands to survive after the Reformation.

Archie took two photographs of the church at different times. The earliest was taken before the demolition of the adjacent blackhouse and construction of the retaining wall, certainly after

1891 as a clock is visible in the tower; it probably dates from 1897, the year of his other dated Castlebay photographs (Fig. 10.5A). A later photograph is dated as after 1901 as the improvement works are not shown on the Ordnance Survey map revised in that year (Fig. 10.5B). The view today is shown in Fig. 10.5C.

Chapter 11

Trade and Comerce

Trade by Sea

We have already seen the importance of steamer routes in the economic development of the islands. Not only were these the only way that people and goods could reach the islands, they were also important for the export of the main products from the islands – namely fish, cattle and wool.

Lochmaddy was the busiest port as it handled traffic not just to the mainland, but provided connections to Tarbert, Lochboisdale and Castlebay. It was also the export port for the cattle droves from North and South Uist and Benbecula. One photograph shows an unusual cargo being loaded (Fig. 11.1) – quite where the pony was bound we do not know!

Fig. 11.1: Shipping a Uist pony at Lochmaddy Pier [*Cairt Phostail* series postcard: 2165; scan courtesy of Norman Hudson].

Fig. 11.2A (right): The Old Pier near Tigh Dearg, Maclean's Mansion on the right [*Cairt Phostail* series postcard: 2124].
Fig. 11.2B (above): The Old Pier in 2007, still in use by local fishing boats. Tigh Dearg has since been restored but the mansion has fallen into disrepair [Photograph: Alastair Chisholm].

Fig. 11.4A (right): Steamer *Dunara Castle* at Loch Skipport [*Cairt Phostail* series postcard: 2403].
Fig. 11.4B (above): Loch Skipport Pier today – no ships call here anymore [Photograph: Michael Cope].

The pier shown in Fig 11.1 was built in the late 1800s to accommodate the growth in steamer traffic and it has been subsequently modified to serve as today's ferry terminal. There is another, older pier in Lochmaddy at Tigh Dearg which was built in the early part of the 19th century as the private landing for the merchant John Maclean, probably c.1800. It became used for smaller traffic with the rise of the steamers and

Fig. 11.3 A, B, C: Three photographs showing the unloading of coal from a boat at the old Lochmaddy Pier in c.1900 with two of Archie's children in the pictures [Original Archie Chisholm photographs: 1166, 1167, 1168; images © NMS].

Pier, Lochskipport, South Uist. (Copyright.)

Fig. 11.5A (right): Cargo and passengers at Loch Skipport [*Cairt Phostail* series postcard: 2402]. Fig. 11.5B (above): Loch Skipport pier today – no cargo or passengers are loaded here anymore [Photograph: Michael Cope].

survives today (Fig. 11.2). A series of three undated photographs show the unloading of coal from a small boat at the old pier (Figs. 11.3 A, B & C). Two of Archie's children accompanied him on this trip, Flora, barefoot, probably aged 6–7 and Helen, three years younger, so dating the photographs as c.1900.

Little is known about the history of the pier at Loch Skipport save that it was developed as an important steamer port built sometime in the late 19th century by Lady Emily Cathcart to service her South Uist Estate. When Archie visited in the early 1900s it appears to have been a thriving port for both export goods and passengers (Figs. 11.4 & 11.5). Terry Williams in her book *Walking with Cattle: in Search of the Last Drovers of Uist* [54] records that the pier was in use until the 1950s for shipment of cattle to the mainland.

Fishing

Sea fishing was a means by which crofters supplemented their food and their income. This was usually undertaken on a collaborative basis of several men taking out a small boat to fish mostly for

Fig. 11.6: Fishermen's houses and boats at Castlebay [Original Archie Chisholm photograph: 1613; image © NMS].

Fishing with a "Tabh" net in Outer Hebrides.   (Copyright)

Fig. 11.7: Fishing with a *tabh* net at Lochmaddy [*Cairt Phostail* series postcard: 2170].

herring and mackerel and sometimes white fish and lobsters. It was difficult work for small boats with the unpredictable Hebridean weather and currents, and ocasional encounters with whales! The way of fishing life in South Uist at the end of the 19th century is described by Angus MacLellan in *The Furrow Behind Me* [55] as 'hard work, cold work and often dangerous work too'. He gives a graphic description of one particularly dangerous trip:

Fig. 11.8: Gutting herring at Castlebay [Original Archie Chisholm photograph: 1616; image © NMS].

One night MacAskill and I were out by ourselves in a little boat, 16 feet long, and it came on bad at sea. We tried to get into an anchorage where we could shelter. When we were only twenty yards outside, it came on a hurricane against us, and we were likely to be blown into the open sea. We were going past a promontory and staying as close to shore as we could and we managed to put down an anchor as we went past the point of the promontory. The anchor held, and we managed to put another out. We sat in the boat all the winter night and neither of us could see the other for spindrift. That was the longest night I ever spent.

A few of Archie's photographs show fishermen's houses, their boats and the fishing itself. Some were taken in Castlebay, Barra – one is shown in Fig. 11.6 (and see the Scottish Home Industries Association postcard Fig. 3.12). Another postcard shows the use of a *tabh* net at Lochmaddy (Fig. 11.7). Erskine Beveridge[8] illustrated and described the construction and use of the *tabh* he observed in North Uist:

....wrought from the root of a grass *Carex flacca* [glaucous sedge] which trails within an inch of the surface and to a length of six to eight feet. This specimen has a one inch mesh and is conical in shape. ... When in use it was placed within a *cabhuil* or dam formed by small stones in the bed of a narrow burn the fish then being driven downstream [into the net].

In the early 19th century larger scale herring fishing became a major industry in Britain with the government giving a bounty to ships over 60 tons and on all catches sold abroad. This, combined with developing railway systems, led to a 'herring boom' and a thriving export trade. The fish were caught all around Britain, especially northern Scotland in the summer months and eastern Scotland in the winter and spring months. The boom peaked in 1907 with 2.5 million barrels of fish exported mostly to Germany, Eastern Europe and Russia.

As part of the growth of the industry the village of Castlebay on Barra was developed as a herring fishery port from 1869 by James Methuen, a master fish-curer from Fife with his main business in Leith.[56] He was one of the first advocates for conservation of fish stocks, promoting through letters to various Scottish newspapers the idea of the need to allow the herring spry to escape capture. He was also vocal about the effects of local petty taxation on both the sale of herring and this being 'injurious to the industrious classes'.

Fig. 11.9A (left): Whaling-Station and whales on stage, Bunamhuinneddor, Harris [*Cairt Phostail* series postcard: 2003].
Fig. 11.9B (above): Ruins of Bunavoneader whaling station today, one of the chimneys still standing [Photograph: Alastair Chisholm].

By the time Archie visited Castlebay in the 1890s it had become a thriving village with around 400 small fishing boats based there (Fig. 9.13). There was also the development of a successful associated fish curing industry, with the labour provided by teams of women known as 'Herring Girls' (Fig. 11.8). The women worked in 'crews' of three – two were gutters and the third was a packer, usually the tallest, who could reach more easily into the packing barrel. Herring Girls developed skills that were in demand throughout Britain. They would follow the fishing with the seasons to work in other parts of the country – sometimes as far away from the Hebrides as Yarmouth in East Anglia.

Whaling at Bunavoneader

The following notes on the history of the whaling station at Bunavoneader, near Ardhasaig, North Harris are taken from an account by David Powell on the *Tasglann nan Eilan Siar* blogsite posted in 2012:[57]

The whaling station at Bunavoneader was first opened by Norwegian father and son Peter and Carl Herlofson, who

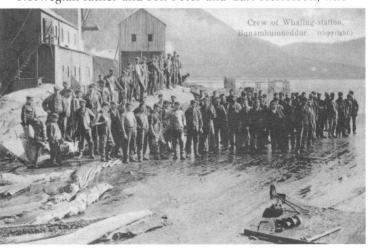

Fig. 11.10A (right): Crew of Whaling-Station, Bunam-huinneddor, Harris [*Cairt Phostail* series postcard: 2004]. Fig. 11.10B (above): The landing stage today [Photograph: Michael Cope].

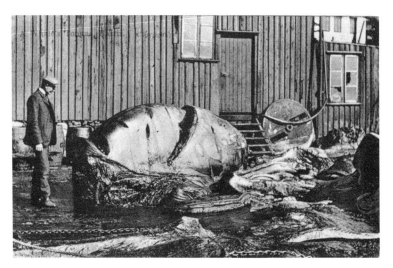

Fig. 11.11: A whale's tongue, Harris [*Cairt Phostail* series postcard: 2005; scan courtesy of Norman Hudson].

founded the company *A/S Harupunen* (The Harpoon). The family had started the company in Iceland in 1896, but were searching for a suitable site further down the North Atlantic, settling on Bunavoneader in 1904. The area had a natural safe harbour and was close to a freshwater stream that supplied both water and generated power for steam saws. Adding to this, it had easy access to the North Atlantic whaling grounds and the markets of Glasgow, making it an ideal site for a whaling station.

The company was so successful that in the years between 1906–1914 it caught the majority of Northern Right whales (so-called as they were the 'right' whale for hunting) caught in Scotland. However, due to the outbreak of WWI, the station was forced to close as the overwhelmingly Norwegian staff were classed as 'aliens', and the few local men employed were called to the war effort.

Archie took three photographs of the station and these must have been taken not long after it opened in 1904 (Figs. 11.9–11.11), probably during the Harris trip of May–June of that year. Today the site is quite derelict, but it remains the most intact example of a whaling station in the northern hemisphere.

Fig. 11.12: Panorama of cattle market at Lochmaddy, undated [Original Archie Chisholm photograph: 1129; Chisholm family collection].

Fig. 11.13: Panorama of cattle market at Lochmaddy, undated [Original Archie Chisholm photograph: 1131; image © NMS].

Fig. 11.14: Panorama of cattle market at Lochmaddy, undated [Original Archie Chisholm photograph: 1130; Chisholm family collection].

Uist Cattle Markets

The cattle markets on the Uists date from the times of droving which began in the 16th century. Cattle and horses were driven across the islands and then through Skye to the mainland to two principal markets known as 'trysts' at Crieff and Falkirk. Along the way 'petty markets' were established as gathering and trading centres – in the Uists these were at Ormacleit on South Uist, Griminish on Benbecula and Lochmaddy on North Uist. According to the *New Statistical Account of Scotland* published in 1845[58] there were two fairs each year, in July and September, for the sale of black cattle and horses in Ormacleit and Lochmaddy.

Fig. 11.15: Cattle market at Lochmaddy, thought to be July 1903 [Original Archie Chisholm photograph: 1133; image © NMS].

Fig. 11.16: Cattle market at Ormacleit, July 1897 [Original Archie Chisholm photograph: 1408; image © NMS].

Fig. 11.17: Cattle market at Ormacleit, July 1897 [Original Archie Chisholm photograph: 1407; image © NMS].

Fig. 11.18: Cattle market at Benbecula, July 1897 [Original Archie Chisholm photograph: 1309; image © NMS].

Fig. 11.19: Cattle market at Benbecula, September 1899 [Original Archie Chisholm photograph: 1310: image © NMS].

Fig. 11.20: Cattle market at Benbecula, September 1899 [Original Archie Chisholm photograph: 1311; image © NMS].

A. R. B. Haldane[33] states that the last droves of island cattle across Skye were made about 1906, and so the trade was still in practice when Archie was in Lochmaddy and photographed by him in those times at Lochmaddy (Figs. 11.12–11.15), Ormacleit (Figs. 11.16 & 11.17) and Benbecula (Figs. 11.18–11.20).

Harris Tweed

Harris Tweed was one of the principal exports of the islands by the late 19th century. The characteristic weave has its origin in the high quality cloth originally produced in the village of Strond, between Obbe and Rodel, by Christine and Marion Macleod (known as the 'Paisley sisters').[59] The quality of the cloth was recognised by the Countess of Dunmore and in 1846 she commissioned the sisters to weave lengths of cloth to her own design which were made up into jackets for the gamekeepers and ghillies on her estate. Subsequently she improved the weaving process and promoted the textile as a fashionable cloth for hunting and sporting wear amongst the aristocracy.

Fig. 11.21A (right):
D. MacAskill, tweed
manufacturer, Tarbert,
Harris [*Cairt Phostail* series
postcard: 2010; scan courtesy
of Norman Hudson].
Fig. 11.21B (above): Former
MacAskill premises today,
now a private residence
[Photograph: Michael Cope].

Across the islands there were commercial outlets for the product and two photographs taken in Tarbert show rolls of cloth outside the premises of D. MacAskill, Tweed Manufacturer, and R. Smith, General Merchant and trader in Harris Tweed. Both buildings survive – the former is a private residence and the latter is now the A. D. Munro Mini-Market (Figs. 11.21 & 11.22);

Fig. 11.22A (right): R. Smith,
trader in Harris Tweed,
Tarbert, Harris [*Cairt Phostail*
series postcard: 2011; scan
courtesy of Norman Hudson].
Fig. 11.22B (below): Former
Smith premises today, now
the A. D. Munro Mini-Market
[Photograph: Michael Cope].

also see Fig. 9.4 which shows the Old Courthouse at Lochmaddy being used as the Scottish Home Industries Association depot for 'Home Spun Tweeds etc.'.

A General Store in North Uist

There is one photograph in the archive titled 'Donald MacLean's shop', without a location, dated April 1897 (Fig 11.23). Some research has determined that this is probably the shop of a Donald MacLean listed as a merchant of Carinish, North Uist in the *Inverness County Directory, 1901*.[60] The sign over the door indistinctly reads 'General Merchant' and the goods outside include what look like rolls of Harris Tweed and several barrels

Fig. 11.23: Donald MacLean's shop, probably Carinish, North Uist, dated April 1897 [Original Archie Chisholm photograph: 1912; image © NMS].

– probably of salted fish. Donald is no doubt the man by the door in the bowler hat and the assembled group is probably his extended family.

Chapter 12

FIELD SPORTS AND PASTIMES

Field Sports Tourism

From the mid 1880s to the outbreak of WW1, coinciding with Archie's residence on the Long Island, there was a 'golden age' of sporting hotels throughout the Highlands and Islands catering for the needs of the wealthier anglers and shots; a pair of the latter make a dramatic appearance in Fig 12.1.[61] On the islands, the main hotels at Tarbert, Rodel, Lochmaddy and Lochboisdale grew to cater for this new breed of tourist attracted mainly by red deer, salmon and trout. The hotels and the fishing and shooting rights were owned by the various estate landlords, who by this time had recognised that the use of land for field sports was at least as, if not more profitable than letting it as sheep farms. The hotels themselves were run by tenants who also leased the associated fishing and shooting rights from the estate owners. Each hotel had its own fishing rivers, lochs and moors and a dedicated staff of gamekeepers and ghillies and so could offer a 'package holiday' inclusive of board, transport and boats – all generally a short distance from the steamer terminal. And it was big business, as David Jones has pointed out in his article for the *Field Sports & Scottish Sporting Gazette*:[62]

> It goes without saying that these angling hotels made an immense contribution to many local economies. For example, in a report dated 1900, the *Daily Express* stated that the six sporting hotels and two fishing inns in the Outer Hebrides alone could 'daily accommodate and find sport for 150 Rods', adding that 'these 150 Rods leave, at least, £1,000 behind them in the Islands for every week spent on their waters'.

Fig. 12.2: Amhuinnsuidhe Castle, North Harris, seat of Sir Samuel Scott [Original Archie Chisholm photograph: 1001; Chisholm family collection].

Red Deer on Shelibost. (Copyright.)

Fig. 12.3: Red deer on The Corran, Seilebost, South Harris [*Cairt Phostail* series postcard: 2017; scan courtesy of Norman Hudson].

Hunting and Fishing

Deer forests were also maintained for the exclusive use of some estate owners and their personal friends rather than tourists. For example, the North Harris Deer Forest became the personal

Fig. 12.1 (facing page): Two hunters with a brace of swans. Unlocated and undated [Original Archie Chisholm photograph: 1901; image © NMS].

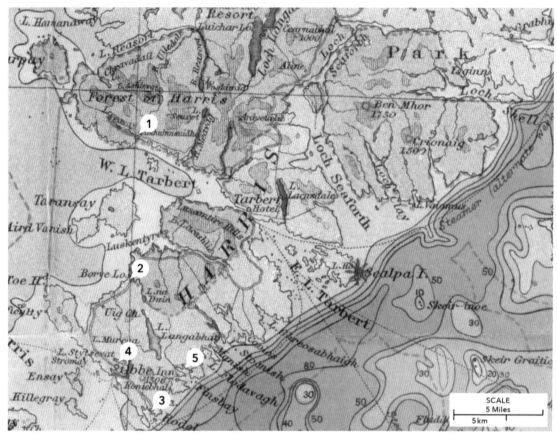

Fig. 12.4: Extract from Bartholomew's *Naturalist's Map of Scotland*, 1893, showing extent of salmon rivers, lochs and deer forest in Harris. Deer forest is shown by the purple shading. Key:
1. Amhuinnsuidhe Castle
2. Borve Lodge
3. Rodel
4. Loch Steisebhat
5. Finsbay.
Reproduced by permission of the NLS.

sporting estate of Sir Edward Scott and was managed from Amhuinnsuidhe Castle (Fig. 12.2) after he acquired the North Harris Estate from the 7th Earl Dunmore in 1871.[62]

By the 1890s a large part of northwestern South Harris had been made over to the Luskentyre Deer Forest owned by the 7th Earl Dunmore and managed from Borve Lodge (Fig. 12.4).[37] We have one photograph of part of its red deer herd at Seilebost on the coast (Fig. 12.3). The remainder of the estate that was not crofted was given over to fishing, especially the rivers and lochs at Obbe, Finsbay and Grosebay; see Fig. 12.4 for locations.

In 1903 a group of Glasgow businessmen founded the

Fig. 12.5A (above): The garden at Rodel Lodge, Archie's wife Helen in the centre of the picture [Original Archie Chisholm photograph: 1045; image © NMS].

Fig. 12.5B (left): Rodel Lodge today (now the Rodel Hotel), renovated in part, but one wing in disrepair. Archie's granddaughter Elizabeth in the centre of the picture [Photograph: Michael Cope].

Fig. 12.6: Landing a boat at Loch Langabhat, Harris [Original Archie Chisholm photograph: 1025; Chisholm family collection].

Hebridean Sporting Association to take leases from the South Harris Estate on the lodge at Rodel, the fishing at Obbe and surrounding lochs, and land at Finsbay on which to build their own fishing lodge. The history of the Association has been described in detail by Michael Gardner in his excellent book *The History of Finsbay Lodge, Harris*.[4] Our particular interest is that Archie was a shareholder in this venture and that Thomas Wilson and his second wife Christina were the major investors and preference shareholders. The Association did not prosper and was wound up in 1922 with mounting debts.

Archie leaves us a contemporary photographic archive relating

Fig. 12.7A left): A favourite cast at Loch Steisebhat, Harris. The fisherman is John Finlayson, gamekeeper at Rodel Lodge [*Cairt Phostail* series postcard: 2036].

Fig. 12.7B (above): Loch Steisebhat today is little changed [Photograph: Michael Cope].

to the Association with images of the fishing on Lochs Langabhat and Steisebhat and the lodges at Rodel and Finsbay (Figs. 12.5– 12.8). Michael Gardner also illustrates the interior of the Finsbay lodge with two of Archie's photographs. It seems most of these photographs were taken on the same trip to Harris in May 1904.

Fishing was not just a sport for tourists, but also a pastime for the local community. F. G. Rea[26] devotes a chapter to how

Fig. 12.8A (left): The Lodge at Finsbay, shortly after construction [*Cairt Phostail* series postcard: 2030].

Fig. 12.8B (below): Site of Finsbay Lodge today. It fell into disrepair in the 1920s and all that remains are the foundations, seen in front of the hut [Photograph: Alastair Chisholm].

Fig. 12.9: Boys fishing, unlocated, probably Uist [Archie Chisholm original photograph: 1914; image © NMS].

he became an enthusiastic river and loch fisherman. When he first arrived in South Uist in 1889, he had no interest in the sport as practised in the ponds and canals of his native English Midlands. His first fishing excursion, with another schoolmaster on the island, was to Loch Hallan, near Daliburgh, South Uist:

> … we set off along the main road [from Daliburgh] towards the north and leaving the township behind us proceeded a mile or so before turning off to the west across a moorland. Quite suddenly we came upon a large loch whose rocky shores gave many bays of deep dark waters…

And, at the end of his day's excursion:

> Needless to say, I was now a complete convert to fishing. … long and serious were our deliberations over the kind of rod I should procure, the casts and the merits of their different makes … Before we parted I had written an order for these from a firm then advertising in the *Fishing Gazette*.

A photograph of Frederick Rea with full fishing tackle taken in 1894 features in his book. From Archie's photographs we have one of schoolboys in Uist fishing at the side of a large loch, but it is unlocated (Fig. 12.9). This photograph was also used in one of the Scottish Home Industries series of postcards (see Chapter 3), so must have been taken before 1903.

Golf on South Uist

Golf originated in Scotland in the 15th century and the standard 18-hole course was first developed at St Andrews in 1764. We have one photograph taken by Archie of a golfing party, complete with

Fig. 12.10: Golfing party, probably at Askernish, South Uist [Original Archie Chisholm photograph: 1414; image © NMS].

'trophies' of bottles of whisky! (Fig. 12.10). As there was only the one golf course on the Uists at the time, we assume it must have been taken at Askernish. The first course in the Outer Hebrides was developed at Stornoway in 1890 and a second developed at Askernish in South Uist in 1891. Its history is documented by the Askernish Golf Club[63] as follows:

> In June 1891 'Old' Tom Morris accompanied by his companion Horace Hutchinson travelled to South Uist at the request of the landowners to inspect the *machair* lands with a view to laying out a new course. 'Old' Tom eventually laid out 18 holes on the rolling dunes of Askernish Farm, although he declared that the choice of links land available was 'staggering'. Horace mentioned the trip in a magazine called *Golf*, the forerunner of *Golf Illustrated*, for which he was to contribute regularly over the next 30 years.

With the tourist boom in the late 19th century, golf links became established across Scotland with *The Golfing Annual* of 1888 listing 126 courses across the country.[64]

Chapter 13

FAIRS AND FESTIVALS

Queen Victoria's Diamond Jubilee 1897

Queen Victoria's Diamond Jubilee on 22nd June 1897 was the first truly nationwide event of her reign and for her subjects the idea of staging such a large public celebration was quite novel. The event was celebrated throughout the British Empire and colonies. The jubilee procession in London was undertaken with due pomp and circumstance and there were parties across the country. By order of the government, and to much disgust from the Temperance Movement, public houses remained open until 2.30 am. A chain of beacons was lit across Britain. The *Inverness Courier* on 25th June 1897 carried reports of the festivities across the Highlands and Islands:

> The Jubilee celebrations throughout the North of Scotland have been characterised by genuine spontaneity and enthusiasm. In every town, village, and parish the day has been observed. The Queen and the members of the Royal Family are not strangers to the Highlands. During the last 50 years, royal visits have been by no means rare. This, perhaps, has added to the heartiness of the demonstrations, as the people feel that they have not themselves been forgotten. It is a characteristic of Highlanders to be loyal, but they are seldom moved to give their loyalty such exuberant expression.

There were no reports of events in Lochmaddy, but a short article referring to Stornoway noted:

> Preparations for the celebration of the Diamond Jubilee were not made on any extensive scale in Stornoway owing to this being

Fig. 13.1: Group outside the Lochmaddy Courthouse on Jubilee Day 22nd June 1897 [Original Archie Chisholm photograph: 1120; image © NMS].

Fig. 13.2: Building the beacon on Blashaval, North Uist [Original Archie Chisholm photograph: 1108; image © NMS].

Fig. 13.3: Building the beacon on Blashaval, North Uist – Archie's hat in the foreground! [Original Archie Chisholm photograph: 1109; image © NMS].

the herring fishing season. ... The town was gaily decorated with bunting by private citizens.

A photograph taken in Lochmaddy on Jubilee day shows not much sign of bunting, but a group is seen outside the Courthouse with flags beneath a banner saying 'God Save the Queen' (Fig. 13.1).

The paper also carried a report of the bonfires lit on the tops of Ben Nevis and Ben Alligin. As part of this national chain a bonfire was also lit on Blashaval in North Uist – Archie had photographed its construction (Figs. 13.2 & 13.3).

Uist Fairs

Over the years the Uist cattle fairs developed into more than just drovers' meeting and trading events. By the late 19th century these had begun to resemble the county shows of today with refreshment and amusement stalls and so became a popular day out for the local population. A series of photographs taken at the fair in July 1903 shows a picnic group (Fig. 13.4) and visitors to the various stalls and tents (Figs. 13.5–13.7). Three postcards were also produced of the fair which it is assumed were taken at the same time (Figs. 13.8–13.10).

Hamish McIlwraith in his online publication *Island Echoes: Voices from North Uist*[65] records the childhood memories of Captain Iain Macdonald from Lochmaddy of the cattle fairs in the early 1900s:

> Oh well, in the very early days of cattle sales there would be always somebody around selling sweeties and things like that. Very little things like sweets. Things to keep the younger set happy because sweets were scarcer. It wasn't every day they could afford a sweetie. It was the sale money. Their father would feel in a generous mood and give his kids a couple of pennies.

Fig. 13.4: Picnic group, probably at Lochmaddy Fair, July 1903 [Original Archie Chisholm photograph: 1913; image © NMS].

As Iain Macdonald was born in 1903, these reminiscences are from several years later than the scenes in Archie's photographs. It is likely, however, that the toys and sweets stalls (Fig. 13.8) were not much changed at that time.

Fig. 13.5: Family group being photographed [Original Archie Chisholm photograph: 1141; image © NMS].

Fig. 13.6: Group in the refreshment tent [Original Archie Chisholm photograph: 1142; image © NMS].

Fig. 13.7: Fairgoers at one of the sales stalls [Original Archie Chisholm photograph: 1140; image © NMS].

Fig. 13.8: Toys and sweets at a Uist Fair [*Cairt Phostail* series postcard: 2139; scan courtesy of Norman Hudson].

Fig. 13.9: Making tea on a Uist Fair [*Cairt Phostail* series postcard: 2134; scan courtesy of Norman Hudson].

Fig. 13.10: Stall at a Uist Market [*Cairt Phostail* series postcard: 2136].

Fig 13.11: View along the Pier Road from the Pier Master's House to the Lochmaddy Hotel – flags and bunting for an event on 18th June 1901 [Original Archie Chisholm photograph: 1162; image © NMS].

Other Events in Lochmaddy

There are a series of photographs dated 18th June 1901 which show several public buildings in Lochmaddy decked out in flags and bunting and a large number of people walking along the road between the pier and the hotel (Figs. 13.11–13.13). Clearly there is something being celebrated, but local enquiries have not identified a specific event in Lochmaddy at this time. Perhaps this was simply advanced preparation for the market and fair in July. Whatever the reason Archie was out and about to record the events.

Fig. 13.12: Pier Master's House, Lochmaddy, taken on 18th June 1901 [Original Archie Chisholm photograph: 1163; image © NMS].

Fig. 13.13: The Bank House, Lochmaddy, taken on 18th June 1901 [Original Archie Chisholm photograph: 1158; image © NMS].

Fig. 13.14A (right): Wedding party at Seilebost, Harris in 1894 [Original Archie Chisholm photograph: 1018; image © NMS; in the SLA collection this photograph is wrongly identified as being located at Luskentyre, Harris]

Fig. 13.14B (above): The remains of the house at Seilebost today [Photograph: Michael Cope].

A Wedding at Seilebost, Harris

There is a single example of Archie as a wedding photographer in 1894 (Fig. 13.14A). This is identified by Michael Gardner[4] as likely being the marriage of Sam Morrison to Christina Stewart – Archie and his colleague Thomas Wilson were the witnesses. The minister (seen in the scarf) was the Reverend Donald McLean of Harris parish. Tony Scherr of Borve Lodge, Harris identifies the house as that of Sam Morrison's parents John and Catherine. It was later used as a weaving shed and visited in 1956 by Queen Elizabeth for a demonstration of weaving of Harris Tweed; the building is now in ruins (Fig. 13.14B).

Chapter 14

Chisholm Family and Home

Family Photographs

After 17 years on the island and a good proportion of that time in temporary accommodation, Archie was finally able to settle in Lochmaddy at Ostrom House in May 1898 with his wife Helen and their then three children Flora (b. 1893), Alexander (b. 1894) and Helen (b. 1896). The earliest photograph of the three children was taken a year earlier in April 1897 near the old pier in Lochmaddy, presumably during a family visit to the island (Fig. 14.1). The same three children were photographed with their mother, probably three years later, likely in winter 1900–1901 (Fig.14.2).

Fig. 14.1: The Chisholm children in April 1897 at Old Tigh Dearg. Helen (in pram) Alexander, centre, and Flora, right [Original Archie Chisholm photograph: 1118; image © NMS].

Fig. 14.2: Helen Chisholm with, from left to right, Flora, Helen and Alexander at Strom Mor Bridge, probably taken by Archie in 1900–1901 [Original Archie Chisholm photograph: 1156; image © NMS].

Fig. 14.3: Tea party game with, left to right, Helen, Mairi, Flora (hidden), Margaret and Alexander, probably taken in 1905 [Original Archie Chisholm photograph: 1155; image © NMS].

Fig. 14.4: Flora sheltering from the sun with her pet dog, probably taken in 1905 [Original Archie Chisholm photograph: 1154; image © NMS].

Fig. 14.5: The six Chisholm children photographed by Archie in Lochmaddy in 1906. From left: Helen (10), Mairi (6), Flora (12), Archibald (2), Margaret (3) and Alexander (11) [Chisholm family collection].

While at Ostrom House three more children were born into the Chisholm family: Mairi (b.1900), Margaret (b.1903) and Archibald (b.1904). Archie gives us a glimpse of the interior of their early Edwardian home with his still life photograph of a gramophone and lily decorations; he also usefully annotates this image with aperture and exposure 'f 3.2, 5 sec' and dates it 8 September 1901 (Fig. 14.8). From previous chapters we have seen that Archie's children used to accompany him on his photographic sorties and feature as subjects in some of his compositions. There are also several photographs in the archive specifically of the children at play in the grounds of Ostrom House – two are shown here (Figs. 14.3–14.4).

We have one photograph of all six children taken by Archie in 1906 (Fig. 14.5); this is the latest surviving photograph from his time in Lochmaddy. Of the six children only Archibald had children of his own, and it is his family, Archie's grandchildren, who have collaborated on the project leading to this book.

Personal Christmas and New Year Greeting Cards

Fig. 14.6: Chisholm family personal Christmas and New Year card 1906–1907 showing Archie's four eldest children, Flora, Alexander, Helen and Mairi, playing outside Ostrom House [Chisholm family collection].

During his time at Ostrom House Archie also produced some Chisholm family personal Christmas and New Year greetings

Fig. 14.7: Chisholm family personal Christmas and New Year card 1903–1904 showing Archie's daughter Mairi [Chisholm family collection].

Mr. and Mrs. Chisholm wish you the Season's Compliments.

OSTROM, Xmas -New Year, 1903-4.

postcards which featured his children as subjects. We have found examples from 1903–1904 and 1906–1907 (Figs. 14.6 & 14.7), but suspect that more are to be found. These cards provide a concluding link between Archie's family life and his commercial venture in producing the *Cairt Phostail* series.

Fig. 14.8: Lilies and gramophone still life composition at Ostrom House [Original Archie Chisholm photograph: 1152; image © NMS].

References and Information Sources

Text References

1   Sir John Orde and the Lochmaddy Procurator Fiscal: Curious Official Revelations. *The Scottish Highlander* 15th February, 22nd February and 1st March 1894.

2   Royal Commission (Highlands and Islands, 1892) (1895) *Minutes of Evidence: Thomas Wilson*. Volume XXXIX, HMSO, London, pp. 1004-1017.

3   Hansard: Commons Sittings: Questions 2nd July 1896, Vol. 42 c523: Official Residence (North Uist). https://api.parliament.uk/historic-hansard/commons/1896/jul/02/official-residence-north-uist.

4   Gardner, M. L. G. (2008) *The History of Finsbay Lodge, Harris: Life and Fishing on a Hebridean Isle*. Self-published, Bradford, England.

5   Charnley, B. (1992) *The Western Isles a Postcard Tour, Vol. 1: Barra to North Uist*. Maclean Press, Isle of Skye, Scotland.

6   Charnley, B. (1992) *The Western Isles a Postcard Tour, Vol. 2: Harris and Lewis*. Maclean Press, Isle of Skye, Scotland.

7   MacKenzie, W. C. (1903) *History of the Outer Hebrides*. Alexander Gardner, Paisley, Scotland.

8   Beveridge, E. (1911) *North Uist: Its Archaeology and Topography*. Birlinn, Edinburgh, Scotland.

9   Fettes, D. J., Mendum, J. R., Smith, D. I., Watson, J. V., Rock, N. M. S. & Mykura, W. (1992). *Geology of the Outer Hebrides*. HMSO, London.

10 Megaw, J. V. S. & Simpson, D.V. A. (1979) *Introduction to British Prehistory*. Leicester University Press, England.

11 Whittow, J. B. (1977) *Geology and Scenery in Scotland*. Penguin Books, England.

12 Barpa Langass, chambered cairn, North Uist. http://portal.historicenvironment.scot/designation/SM892.

13 Sornach Coir'Fhinn, stone circle. http://portal.historicenvironment.scot/designation/SM5125.

14 Gazetteer for Scotland: Clach Mhor a Che. http://www.scottish-places.info/features/featurefirst20637.html.

15 News from the Department of Archaeology at the University of Reading. https://blogs.reading.ac.uk/archaeology.

16 North Uist, Loch Aonghais, Dun Aonais. https://canmore.org.uk/site/10366/north-uist-loch-aonghais-dun-aonais.

17 Barra, Dun Mhic Leoid. https://canmore.org.uk/site/21394/barra-dun-mhic-leoid.

18 Benbecula, Borve Castle. https://canmore.org.uk/site/9962/benbecula-borve-castle.

19 Stack Islands, Eilean Leathan, Weaver's Castle. https://canmore.org.uk/site/9763/stack-islands-eilean-leathan-weavers-castle.

20 North Uist, Carinish, Teampull Na Trionaid. https://canmore.org.uk/site/10265/north-uist-carinish-teampull-na-trionaid.

21 South Uist, Benbecula, Balivanich, Teampall Chaluim Chille. https://canmore.org.uk/site/9970/south-uist-benbecula-balivanich-teampall-chaluim-chille.

22 Lawson, B. (2002). *Harris in History and Legend*. Birlinn, Edinburgh, Scotland.

23 Lawson, B. (1991). *St Clement's Church at Rodel*. Bill Lawson Publications, Isle of Harris.

24 Johnson, S. (1775, ed. P. Levi, 1964) *A Journey to the Western Islands of Scotland*. Penguin Classics, Middlesex, England.

25 Hunter, J. (2000) The *Making of the Crofting Community*. Birlinn, Edinburgh, Scotland.

26 Rea, F. G. (1964, ed. J. L. Campbell 1997) *A School in South Uist: Reminiscences of a Hebridean School Master 1890-1913*. Birlinn, Edinburgh, Scotland.

27 Lawson, B. (2004) *North Uist in History and Legend*. John Donald, Edinburgh, Scotland.

28 Mackay, J. A. (1978) *Islands Postal History Series No.1: Harris & St. Kilda*. Self-published, Dumfries, Scotland.

29 Mackay, J. A. (1978) *Islands Postal History Series No.2: The Uists & Barra*. Self-published, Dumfries, Scotland.

30 Mackay, J. A. (1978) *Islands Postal History Series No.3: Lewis*. Self-published, Dumfries, Scotland.

31 MacBrayne, David (1884) *Official Guide to Summer Tours in Scotland:*

Glasgow to the Highlands 'Royal Route'. Glasgow, Scotland.

32 Goodrich-Freer, A. (1902) *Outer Isles*. Constable & Co, London.

33 Haldane, A. R. B. (1952) *The Drove Roads of Scotland*. Thomas Nelson & Sons, London, England.

34 North Ford Causeway. https://www.cne-siar.gov.uk/roads-travel-and-parking/bridges-causeways-and-ferries/north-ford-causeway.

35 Burnett, R. (1986) *Benbecula*. Mingulay Press, Isle of Benbecula, Scotland.

36 SUE Archive: 5. Inns and Hotels. https://prodigia.files.wordpress.com/2008/08/05-inns-and-hotels.pdf.

37 Scherr, T. (2017) *A History of Borve Lodge*. Self-published, Isle of Harris, Scotland.

38 The Scotsman 10th March 2017. http://www.scotsman.com/news/when-a-hebridean-island-got-its-first-motor-car-1-4389213.

39 Kennedy-Fraser, M. (1929) *A Life in Song*. Oxford University Press, England.

40 Taubman, A. (2009) *Electric Telegraph to e-Scotland: Networking remote and rural communities*. In: K. Veitch (ed.) *A Compendium of Scottish Ethnology Volume 8: Transport and Communications*. John Donald, Edinburgh, Scotland, pp. 728-748.

41 Friday Photo: the Marconi Pole 14th June 2013. http://blogserver.cne-siar.gov.uk/wp-archivist/?p=2496.

42 Census of Scotland Population Reports: 1881, 1891, 1901 &1911. http://www.histpop.org.

43 Hutchinson, R. (2003) *The Soap Man: Lewis, Harris and Lord Leverhulme*. Birlinn, Edinburgh, Scotland.

44 Lochmaddy. http://www.undiscoveredscotland.co.uk/northuist/lochmaddy.

45 North Uist, Lochmaddy, Maclean's Mansion. https://canmore.org.uk/site/300929/north-uist-lochmaddy-macleans-mansion.

46 National Library of Scotland Digital Resources: Maps and Gazetteers of Scotland 1803-1901. http://digital.nls.uk.

47 Castlebay. https://www.undiscoveredscotland.co.uk/barra/castlebay.

48 Kilmuir Church, North Uist. https://www.scotlandschurchestrust.org.uk/church/kilmuir-church-north-uist.

49 *Stornoway Gazette* 13th November 2008: Facelift for St Mary's to mark 125 years. http://www.stornowaygazette.co.uk/news/facelift-for-st-mary-s-to-mark-125-years-1-120585 .

50 South Uist, Daliburgh, St Peter's RC Church. https://canmore.org.uk/site/171992/south-uist-daliburgh-st-peters-rc-church.

51 South Uist, Eriskay, St Michael's Roman Catholic Church. https://canmore.org.uk/site/172006/south-uist-eriskay-st-michaels-roman-catholic-church.

52 Hutchinson, R. (2010) *Father Allan: The Life and Legacy of a Hebridean Priest*. Birlinn, Edinburgh, Scotland.

53 Barra Catholic Church: The Barra Catholic Diocese of Argyll and the Isles. https://barracatholic.co.uk.

54 Williams, T. J. (2017) *Walking with Cattle: in Search of the Last Drovers of Uist*. Birlinn, Edinburgh, Scotland.

55 MacLellan, A. transl. J. L. Campbell (1997) *The Furrow Behind Me*. Birlinn, Edinburgh, Scotland.

56 Scottish Continental Herring Trade 1810–1914. http://www.scottishherringhistory.uk/1809-1881/Methuen.html.

57 Friday Photo: Bunavoneader whaling station 10th August 2012. http://blogserver.cne-siar.gov.uk/wp-archivist/?p=1971.

58 New Statistical Account of Scotland (1845): Volume 14 Inverness – Ross and Cromarty. https://www.electricscotland.com/history/statistical/volume14.htm.

59 Hebridean Connections: Real People Real Lives: The History of Harris Tweed. http://www.hebrideanconnections.com/stories-reports-and-traditions/38018.

60 Internet Archive Digital Library: Inverness County Directories 1887-1920. https://archive.org.

61 Jones, D. S. D. (2006) 'A Spot for One's Sport: from 19th century sportsmen's retreats to 21st century resorts'. *Field Sports & Scottish Sporting Gazette* Summer 2016. https://www.fieldsportsmagazine.com/Scottish-Culture/a-spot-for-ones-sport.html.

62 Jones, D. S. D. (2011) *Amhuinnsuidhe and North Harris: The History of an Outer Hebridean Sporting Estate*. Self-published, Fovant, England.

63 Askernish Golf Club: History & Restoration. http://www.askernishgolfclub.com.

64 Scottish Golf History.http://www.scottishgolfhistory.org/oldest-golf-courses/.

65 Island Echoes: Voices from North Uist. https://www.taigh-chearsabhagh.org/wp-content/uploads/2014/08/Island-Echoes-Voices-from-North-Uist.pdf.

Other Reference and Information Sources

British Newspaper Archive. https://www.britishnewspaperarchive.co.uk.

Electric Scotland: History and Culture of Scotland. http://www.electricscotland.com.

Gazetteer for Scotland. http://www.scottish-places.info

Linguae Celticae: Gàidhlig (Scottish Gaelic) Local Studies. http://www.linguae-celticae.org

Miers, M. (2008) *The Western Seaboard: An Illustrated Architectural Guide.* (RIAS Series of Architectural Guides to Scotland). Rutland Press, England.

Parker-Pearson, M., Sharples, N. & Symonds, J. (2004) *South Uist: Archaeology and History of a Hebridean Island.* Tempus, Stroud, England.

Places of Worship in Scotland. http://www.scottishchurches.org.uk.

Royal Bank of Scotland Heritage Hub. https://www.rbs.com/heritage/places.

Scotland's People: National Records of Scotland: Census Records and Statutory Registers. https://www.scotlandspeople.gov.uk.

Taigh Chearsabhagh (1996) *Between Two Worlds: Lochmaddy 1600–1995.* (Booklet to accompany exhibition *Eadar Da Shaoghal* held at Taigh Chearsabhagh, Lochmaddy, North Uist, March–December 1995).

Appendix 1

Locations of Photographs and Picture Postcards

As far as possible all of the locations of Archie's photographs have been researched in the field. Where locations are fully identified these have been authenticated in *Google Earth*™ and converted to National Grid References with 10m accuracy (eight figures) using the web-based Batch Convert Tool (www.gridreferencefinder.com); for less precisely identified locations grid references to 100m accuracy (six figures) are quoted. In the case of locations where only a general area is known and multiple photographs exist (e.g. market stances) a kilometre grid square quadrant is specified. Where known, the dates the images were taken are listed.

For some images it is simply not possible to identify a location with any degree of certainty. In some cases the caption or manuscript note provides an approximate location, in others a possible island location is suggested by the author. It is acknowledged that readers of this book might be able to identify some of the unlocated images and the author would be grateful to receive appropriate corrections via the publisher.

In Tables A.1 – A.7 a unique reference number is assigned to each image using the following conventions:

1. Photographs are identified with the prefix '1', *Cairt Phostail* picture postcards with the prefix '2' and other illustrated postcards with the prefix '3'.
2. Images are arranged north to south and assigned appropriate sequence numbers: Harris (001–099), North Uist (101–299), Benbecula (301–399), South Uist (401–499), Eriskay (501–599) and Barra (601–699).
3. Unlocated or out of area images are assigned sequence numbers 901–999.

4. In the case of photographs and postcards that show differences in their captions, colour tint or scale of view, but are otherwise the same image, the suffixes 'A', 'B' etc. are used.

Where appropriate the catalogue numbers of images in the Scottish Life Archive of the National Museum of Scotland (SLA/NMS) are also shown.

In the tables the original spellings of place names as recorded on photographic prints in Archie's manuscript notes or the printed captions on picture postcards have been retained. It is acknowledged that this does lead to some anomalies in Gaelic translations, such as his use of *Loch-an-madaidh* and *Loch-na-madaidh* instead of *Loch-nam-Madadh* for Lochmaddy and *Uidhist* instead of *Uibhist* for Uist. It is considered, however, that historical accuracy of the original document should be preserved.

As far as possible the photographic locations are represented graphically on extracts from Ordnance Survey One-Inch and Six-Inch scale maps published between 1896 and 1904, these being current with Archie's main photographic period (Figs. A.1–A.16); all are reproduced by permission of the National Library of Scotland; location icons for each figure are courtesy www.d-maps.com.

TABLE A.1: LOCATIONS OF PHOTOGRAPHS AND PICTURE POSTCARDS - HARRIS

ef No	Type	SLA/NMS Cat No	Title or Description	Date	Nat Grid Ref
1001	Print		Amhuinnsuidh Castle, North Harris, Seat of Sir Samuel Scott	-	NB 0484 0777
002	Print		From Strone Ardhasaig - Ardhasaig looking west, North Harris	-	NB 1315 0298
003	PC		Whaling-Station, and whales on stage, Bunamhuinneddor	-	NB 1301 0420
004	PC		Crew of Whaling-station, Bunamhuinneddor [Caption upper right]	-	NB 1307 0404
004A	PC		Crew of Whaling-station, Bunamhuinneddor [Caption lower central]	-	NB 1307 0404
005	PC		A Whale's Tongue, Harris	-	NB 130 040
006	Print	C1731	Sgaoth Iosal and road from Ardhasaig, North Harris	1902-10-27	NG 0419 9187
006	PC		Scaw, Ardhasaig [Caption upper right]	-	NB 1361 0338
006A	PC		The Scaw, from Strone, Ardhasaig, Harris [Caption upper central]	-	NB 1361 0338
007	PC		West Loch Tarbert, Harris	-	NB 1487 0026
008	PC		Tarbert, West	-	NB 1516 0010
009	PC		The Hotel, Tarbert, Harris, Scotland	-	NB 1526 0008
010	PC		Tarbert, Harris, Scotland [D MacAskill, Tweed Manufacturer]	-	NB 1541 0001
011	PC		Tarbert, Harris, Scotland [R Smith, General Merchant]	-	NG 1576 9995
012	PC		East Loch Tarbert, looking to Scalpay, Harris	-	NG 1567 9992
013	PC		Pier (East), Tarbert, Harris	-	NG 1576 9986
014	PC		East Pier, and Tarbert, Harris	-	NG 1576 9983
015	PC		Tarbert, Harris	-	NG 1544 9986
016	Print	53-24-43	Looking north from Namh-ard, South Harris		NG 1451 9801
017	PC		Red Deer on Shelibost	-	NG 0627 9749
018	Print	C3558	Wedding party at Seilebost, South Harris	1894-??-??	NG 0623 9711
019	Print	C29402	Southeast side of Loch Plocropol, South Harris	1904-05-31	NG 1782 9362
020	Print	C29401	Crofter's house, Plocropol, South Harris	1904-05-31	-
020	PC		A Hillside Croft in picturesque Harris [Plochropol]	-	-
021	Print	C29400	Creag, Scadabay, South Harris	1904-05-31	NG 1707 9243
021	PC		'An Creag', Scadabay, a Crofting Township View, Outer Hebrides	-	NG 1707 9243
022	Print		Sunset at Head of Collam Bay Grosebay, South Harris	1904-05-31	NG 1540 9132
023	Print		Loch Grosebay, South Harris	1904-05-31	NG 1556 9123
023	PC		Loch Grosebay, Harris	-	NG 1556 9123
024	Print		Loch Langabhat, South Harris from north end	1904-05-27	NG 0419 9187
025	Print		A landing place at Langabhat, South Harris	1904-05-27	NG 0445 8907

1026	Print		Marsh Bean, Buck Bean at Loch an rathaid more, Finsbay, South Harris	1904-05-30	NG 0902 8820
1027	Print		Marsh Bean, Tri-bhileach, on Loch an rathaid more, Finsbay, South Harris	1904-05-30	NG 0901 8821
1028	Print		Corner of Smoke Room, Finsbay Lodge, South Harris	1904-06-01	NG 0826 8749
1029	Print		'Oriel' in Dining Room, Finsbay Lodge, South Harris	1904-06-01	NG 0827 8750
1030	Print		Finsbay Lodge from south side, South Harris	1904-06-02	NG 0822 8714
2030	PC		Finsbay Hotel, South Harris	-	NG 0822 8714
1031	Print	54-27-21A	Finsbay Lodge, South Harris	-	NG 0817 8718
1032	Print		Finsbay Lodge, South Harris	1904-06-02	NG 0835 8702
1033	Print		Finsbay Lodge from south, South Harris [Four men in a boat in foreground]	1904-06-02	NG 0826 8712
1034	Print	C1713	Cottar's house, Finsbay, South Harris	1904-06-01	NG 0811 8721
1035	Print	C1704	Peat cutting – Donald & Malcolm MacAskill, cottars, Obbe at Rhu Mhhearlich, Steishabhat, South Harris	1904-05-27	NG 0208 8850
2035	PC		Peat-Casting in the Outer Hebrides	-	NG 0208 8850
1036	Print	C1703	On Steishabhat, north side of west wing at Am Picar Finlayson fishing, South Harris	1904-05-27	NG 0137 8787
2036	PC		A favourite cast, Outer Hebrides [Caption at top]	-	NG 0137 8787
2036A	PC		A favourite Cast, in Outer Hebrides [Caption at bottom]	-	NG 0137 8787
2037	PC		An t-Ob, 's na Herradh	-	NG 0231 8652
1037	Print	C3559	Obbe, South Harris	1903-11-17	NG 0225 8657
1038	Print	54-27-20A	Obbe, South Harris	1900-??-??	NG 0231 8652
1039	Print	C1706	Crofters corn-sowing at Obbe and the Obbe loch, South Harris	1904-05-28	NG 0213 8648
1040	Print		Pigeon Cave on sea between Rodel and Finsbay, South Harris	1904-05-30	NG 0852 8551
2041	PC		In Rodel Wood	-	NG 0422 8405
1042	Print	C29395	St Clements, Rodel, South Harris [View from northeast]	c 1903-11-19	NG 0484 832C
2042	PC		St Clement's Rodel, from the North [Caption at top]	-	NG 0484 832C
2042A	PC		St Clement's Rodel, from the North [Caption at bottom]	-	NG 0484 832C
1043	Print	C29394	St Clements, Rodel, South Harris [View from southwest]	c 1903-11-19	NG 0478 8312
2044	PC		Tomb of Alasdair Crotach, St Clement's Rodel	-	NG 0478 8317
1045	Print	C29393	Garden at Rodel Hotel, South Harris [Woman in foreground]	-	NG 0474 8285
2045	PC		Rodel Hotel, South Harris	-	NG 0474 8285
1046	Print	54-27-22A	Rodel Hotel, South Harris [View from island]	-	NG 0479 8274
1047	Print	C29397	Rodel Hotel, South Harris [View from island]	1904-06-02	NG 0479 827
1048	Print	C29396	Rodel Hotel, South Harris [View from jetty]	-	NG 0488 828.
1049	Print	53-24-27	View from boat towards coast at Rodel, South Harris	-	NG 0427 827.
2050	PC		Picturesque Harris, Storm on Ru Vollarip	-	NG 0564 830

TABLE A 2: LOCATIONS OF PHOTOGRAPHS AND PICTURE POSTCARDS - NORTH UIST

Ref No	Type	SLA/ NMS Cat No	Title or Description	Date	Nat Grid Ref
1101	Print	C1708	At Rishgarry Quay, Berneray, Harris	1904-07-17	NF 9257 8193
2101	PC		In Berneray of Harris	-	NF 9257 8193
2102	PC		Cladh Maelrubha, Berneray, Harris	-	NF 9123 8070
2103	PC		Newton Ferry [Telegraph Office]	-	NF 8950 7837
2104	PC		Hougarry	-	NF 9172 6864
2105	PC		Dun Aonghais us an Crogair	-	NF 8545 7382
2106	Print	C1631	Gerron Mill, North Uist	1897-04-??	NF 8441 7352
2107	PC		Lochportan, Loch-na-madaidh	-	NF 9534 7141
2108	Print	C1674	Diamond Jubilee Bonfire on Blashaval, North Uist	1897-06-??	NF 8920 7146
2109	Print	C1679	Diamond Jubilee Bonfire, Blashaval, North Uist [Archie's hat foreground]	1897-06-??	NF 8920 7146
2110	PC		Sponish House	-	NG 1707 9243
2111	Print		Rowing boat in inlet near Struth Mhor, Creagorry Mhor in background	-	-
2112	Print	C29398	Lochmaddy from roadside near Struth Mhor [Distance view]	1902-10-10	NF 9116 6906
2113	Print	C29399	Lochmaddy from roadside near school [Close-up view]	1902-10-10	NF 9152 6874
2114	PC		Buain corc, an Loch-an-madaidh	-	NF 9118 6916
2115	PC		Tighean Cruitearan, Uidhist-a-tuath	-	-
2116	PC		Lochmaddy [Under snow]	-	NF 9169 6898
2117	PC		Am Poste Office, an Loch-na-Madadh	-	NF 9181 6895
2118	Print	C1719	Girls and baby in pram, Old Tigh Dearg, Lochmaddy	1897-04-??	NF 9189 6879
2119	PC		County Buildings, Lochmaddy	-	NF 9181 6890
2120	Print	C1686	Diamond Jubilee group, New Court House, Lochmaddy	1897-06-??	NF 9179 6889
2121	Print	C1733	Group with bicycles etc , outside New Court House, Lochmaddy	-	NF 9179 6889
2122	PC		[Old Court House – no caption on front]	-	NF 9178 6889
2123	PC		And Her Grace the Duchess of Sutherland, in front [of Old Courthouse]	-	NF 9178 6889
2124	PC		Sean Laimhrig s buth Iain Domhnullach an Loch-na-madaidh	-	NF 9187 6884
2125	PC		Sean Laimhrig agus Tigh-na-Cuirte etc Loch-na-madhaidh	-	NF 9205 6879
2126	PC		Lochmaddy, School	-	NF 9150 6875
2127	PC		An Loch na madaidh	-	NF 9154 6874
2128	PC		Lochmaddy from Market stance	-	NF 9106 6911
2129	Print		Cattle Show, Lochmaddy	-	NF 9169 SW
2130	Print		Cattle Show, Lochmaddy	-	NF 9169 SW

1131	Print	C1693	Market, Lochmaddy	1903-07-??	NF 9169 SW
1132	Print	C1710	Market Stance, Lochmaddy	-	NF 9169 SW
1133	Print	C1700	Market Stance, Lochmaddy	-	NF 9169 SW
2133	PC		Feill a Loch-na-madaidh [Cattle]	-	NF 9169 SW
2134	PC		Making tea on a Uist fair	-	NF 9169 SW
2135	PC	45-7-22	A Uist Market I	-	NF 9169 SW
2136	PC		A Uist Market II	-	NF 9169 SW
2137	PC		Feill a' Loch-na-madaidh [People and horses]	-	NF 9169 SW
2138	PC		Air feill an Uidhist	-	NF 9169 SW
2139	PC		Toys and Sweets at a Uist fair	-	NF 9169 SW
1140	Print	C240B	Lochmaddy Market [Figures and booth]	-	NF 9169 SW
1141	Print	C241B	Lochmaddy Market [Photographer and group posing]	-	NF 9169 SW
1142	Print	C243	Lochmaddy Market [Figures in a tent]	-	NF 9169 SW
1143	Print	C1673	Lochmaddy Market [Figures in a drinking tent, horse on right]	-	NF 9169 SW
1144	Print	C1724	Lochmaddy Market [Photographer at work]	-	NF 9169 SW
1145	Print	C240a	Pier Master at Lochmaddy Market	1903-07-??	NF 9169 SW
1146	Print	C4304	Eviction, Kate McDiarmid's house, Lochmaddy [Two men carrying barrel]	-	NF 9174 6884
1147	Print	C1711	Eviction, Kate McDiarmid's house, Lochmaddy [Two men at door]	-	NF 9174 6884
1148	Print	C4303	Eviction, Kate McDiarmid's house, Lochmaddy [Two men carrying bench]	-	NF 9174 6884
1149	Print	C1712	Eviction, Kate McDiarmid's house, Lochmaddy [Furniture outside house]	-	NF 9174 6884
1150	Print	C1707	Eviction, Kate McDiarmid's house, Lochmaddy [Two men and furniture outside house]	-	NF 9174 6884
1151	Print	C4301	Eviction, Kate McDiarmid's house, Lochmaddy [Girls outside house]	-	NF 9174 6884
1152	Print	C1699	Interior, Ostrom, Lochmaddy [Still life with exposure details f 32, 5 m]	1901-09-08	NF 9178 6877
1153	Print	C1734	Children playing, Ostrom House, Lochmaddy [Two children with tea-cup]	1903-07-27	NF 9179 6877
1154	Print	C1728	Children playing, Ostrom House, Lochmaddy [Girl with umbrella and dog]	1903-07-27	NF 9179 6877
1155	Print	C1678	Five children playing, Ostrom House, Lochmaddy [with miniature tea set]	1903-07-27	NF 9179 6877
1156	Print	C1717	Chisholm Family group on bridge in snow, Lochmaddy	-	NF 9064 6962
2157	PC		Lochmaddy, Bank of Scotland	-	NF 9173 6866
1158	Print	C1684	Bankhouse, Lochmaddy	1901-06-18	NF 9170 6856
1159	Print		View of bay from Bankhouse, Lees in background, Lochmaddy	-	NF 9172 6864
2160	PC		Lochmaddy	-	NF 9182 6853
2161	PC		Lochmaddy Hotel, Lochmaddy (D Macfadyen, Proprietor)	-	NF 9197 6821
1162	Print	C1685	Pier Master's House and Hotel, Lochmaddy	1901-06-18	NF 9203 6805

1163	Print	C1680	Pier Master's House, Lochmaddy	1901-06-18	NF 9201 6809
1164	Print	C1732	Steamer arriving at Lochmaddy Pier	-	NF 9204 6798
2165	PC		Shipping a Uist Pony	-	NF 9202 6800
1166	Print	C1692	Unloading coal, Lochmaddy Pier	1903-06-22	NF 9190 6880
1167	Print	C1697	Unloading coal, Lochmaddy Pier	1903-06-22	NF 9190 6880
1168	Print	C1694	Unloading coal, Lochmaddy Pier	1903-06-22	NF 9190 6880
1169	Print	C1714	Crofts Strombane, Lochmaddy	-	NF 9211 6740
2170	PC		Fishing with a "Tabh" net in Outer Hebrides [Lees in background]	-	-
1171	Print	C4638	The Smithy, Lochmaddy	1892-04-??	NF 9132 6889
1172	Print		The Smithy, Lochmaddy - [Image reversed]	-	NF 9132 6889
1173	Print		Lochmaddy, North Uist with Crogearraidh Mor in background	-	NF 9288 6738
2173	PC		Loch-na-madaidh bho Lee	-	NF 9288 6738
2174	PC		Lochmaddy from top of Lee	-	NF 9270 6602
2175	PC		Air Loch-na-madaidh	-	NF 9430 6908
1176	Print		Lochmaddy from below Lees, man and three children sitting in boat	-	NF 9284 6743
1177	Print	C1721	? Horses and soldiers, Lochmaddy	1903-06-22	-
2178	PC		Parish Church of North Uist	-	NF 7268 7016
2179	PC		Creag Hastin, North Uist	-	NF 7395 6717
2180	PC		Balaranuill Uidhist-a-tuath	-	NF 7268 6963
2181	PC		Clach a Che and Dun, Claddach-Kirkibost, North Uist	-	NF 7698 6618
2182	PC		Westford Inn, by Lochmaddy	-	NF 7748 6622
1183	Print	C1688	At Cladach Kyles, North Uist [Blackhouses, peat stack and cart in front]	1897-05-10	NF 7766 SW
1184	Print	C1720	Cladach Illeray, North Uist [Family and cow in front of blackhouse]	1897-04-??	NF 7964 SE
1185	Print	C1715	Cladach Illeray, North Uist [Man, horse and cart in front of blackhouse]	1897-04-??	NF 7964 SE
2186	PC		Clachan, Locheport	-	NF 8107 6392
2187	PC		Clachan, Locheport, Shop of Mr Ferguson and Post Office	-	NF 8105 6399
1188	Print	C1690	Roup at FC Minister's House, Clachanaghluib, North Uist	1897-04-??	NF 8114 6377
1189	Print	C1675	Sale at late Mr MacAlpine's, Clachanaghluib, North Uist	1897-??-??	NF 8114 6377
190	PC		Langash Lodge	-	NF 8391 6514
2191	PC		Ancient Stone Circle, Langash	-	NF 8431 6499
192	PC		Barp, Langass, Uidhist-a-tuath [Caption at bottom]	-	NF 8381 6572
92A	PC		Barp, Langass [Caption at top]	-	NF 8381 6572
193	PC	56-11-19	An Tigh-Osda, Carinish	-	NF 8215 6032

191

2194	PC		An Tigh-osda, Carinish, Uidhist-a-tuath	-	NF 8217 6029
2195	PC		Trinity Temple from North	-	NF 8161 6031
2196	PC		Trinity Temple from South	-	NF 8162 6025
2197	PC		Teampull na Trionaid, Carinish	-	NF 8162 6025
1198	Print		Trinity Church, Carinish, North Uist	-	NF 8165 6026
2199	PC		Entrance to the North Ford at Carinish	-	NF 8244 6001
2200	PC		End of North Ford and Carinish	-	NF 8240 6004
2201	PC		HM Mails on North Ford	-	-
2203	PC		Evening on a Uist Sea Ford	-	-
2204	PC		Seann Phriosann agus Tigh-na-Cuirte an Loch-na-madaidh	-	NF 9182 6884
3205	PC		Ostrom, Lochmaddy	-	NF 9178 6881

TABLE A.3: LOCATIONS OF PHOTOGRAPHS AND PICTURE POSTCARDS - BENBECULA

Ref No.	Type	SLA/NMS Cat No.	Title or Description	Date	Nat Grid Ref
2301	PC		Cille-Chalumcille, Benbecula.	-	NF 7823 5490
2302	PC		Beinn-na-faoghla, Eaglais Cnoc-Mhorra, agus Tigh-chleir.	-	NF 7784 5202
2303	PC	45-7-14	Ruins of Dun, Borve, Benbecula, from the North. [Note: image reversed]	-	NF 7734 5054
2304	PC	45-7-17	Ruins of Dun, Borve, Benbecula, from South. [Large image]	-	NF 7734 5050
2304A	PC		Ruins of Dun, Borve, Benbecula, from South. [Small image]	-	NF 7694 5026
1305	Print	C1729	Creagorry Post Office, Benbecula	1903-08-10	NF 7963 4890
2305	PC		Benbecula. [Creagorry Post Office]	-	NF 7963 4890
2306	PC		Creagorry Hotel, Benbecula. (A. MacLean, Proprietor)	-	NF 7972 4850
2307	PC	C-5249	Creagorry, and hills of South Uist	-	NF 7970 4857
2308	PC		From Creagorry, the South Ford and South Uist	-	NF 7991 4803
1309	Print	C1676	Benbecula Market [Figures and booths - woman in plaid]	1897-07-??	NF 8053 NE
1310	Print	C1702	Benbecula Market [Figures and horses - carriage at right]	1897-09-??	NF 8053 NE
1311	Print	C1722	Benbecula Market [Figures and horses - rider at right]	1897-09-??	NF 8053 NE

TABLE A.4: LOCATIONS OF PHOTOGRAPHS AND PICTURE POSTCARDS - SOUTH UIST

Ref No.	Type	SLA/NMS Cat No.	Title or Description	Date	Nat Grid Ref
2401	PC		South Ford and Benbecula from Carnan	-	NF 7996 4684
2402	PC		Pier, Lochskipport, South Uist	-	NF 8295 3863
2403	PC		Lochskipport, South Uist	-	NF 8290 3865
2404	PC		Post Office, Howmore	-	NF 7681 3450
2405	PC		Bute Hospital, Dalibrog, South Uist	-	NF 7562 2133
2406	PC		Eaglais Chaitliceach 'us Tigh an t-Sagairt, Dhalibrog	-	NF 7453 2104
2407	Print	C242B	Ormiclate Market, South Uist	1897-07-??	NF 7631 SW
2408	Print	C241A	Ormiclate Market, South Uist	1897-07-??	NF 7631 SW
2409	PC		Lochboisdale [view to NW]	-	NF 7927 1935
2410	PC		Lochboisdale [view to SE]	-	NF 7915 1945
2411	PC		Lochboisdale Hotel, South Uist, by Oban Simon Mackenzie, Proprietor	-	NF 7937 1937
2412	PC		Lochboisdale, 'Marconi' pole	-	NF 7923 1947
2413	Print	C358	Man ploughing with pair of horses plus cleric and dog, South Uist	-	-
2413	PC		Treabhadh 'n Uidhist-a-deas	-	-
2414	Print	C1687	Group of golfers [probably at Askernish]	-	NF 730 240

Ref No.	Type	SLA/NMS Cat No.	Title or Description	Date	Nat Grid Ref
2501	PC		An t-Urramach Maighstir Ailean 'us am Pobull an deidh n' aifrionn, an Eriskay	-	NF 7868 1201
2502	PC		Post Office, Eriskay [Caption upper right]	-	NF 7908 1193
2502A	PC		The Post Office, Eriskay, Outer Hebrides [Caption upper central]	-	NF 7908 1193
2503	PC	C5246	Bala, Eriskay, where Prince Charlie first slept in Britain [B&W]	-	NF 7835 1171
2503A	PC		Bala, Eriskay, where Prince Charlie first slept in Britain [Colour]	-	NF 7835 1171
2504	PC		Eriskay, spot where Prince Charlie first landed in Britain for the '45 [B&W]	-	NF 7844 1106
2504A	PC		Eriskay, spot where Prince Charlie first landed in Britain for the '45 [Colour]	-	NF 7844 1106
2504B	PC		Prince Charlie's Landing, Eriskay [Enlargement]	-	NF 7844 1106
2505	PC		Prince Charlie's first landing-place in Britain for the '45 [B&W]	-	NF 7846 1104
2505A	PC		Prince Charlie's first landing-place in Britain for the '45 [Colour]	-	NF 7846 1104
2506	PC		In Bala, Eriskay, where Prince Charlie slept first night in Britain [Colour]	-	NF 7849 1154
2507	PC		Dun, Staak-a-Bhreabadair, Sound of Barra	-	NF 7856 0725

TABLE A.6: LOCATIONS OF PHOTOGRAPHS AND PICTURE POSTCARDS -BARRA

Ref No.	Type	SLA/NMS Cat No.	Title or Description	Date	Nat Grid Ref
2601	PC		At Halaman, Barra	-	NF 6471 0046
2602	PC		Lochmor us Dun Mhicleoid	-	NL 6490 9961
2603	PC		Kentangval [Road looking south]	-	NL 6549 9889
2604	PC		Kentangval [Road looking north]	-	NL 6561 9865
2605	Print	C1682	Kentangval, Barra [Blackhouses]	1901-11-06	-
2606	PC		Castlebay	-	NL 6618 9842
2607	Print		Castlebay and Kisimul Castle, Barra	-	NL 6653 9833
2608	PC		Bagh a' Chaisteal, Barraigh	-	NL 6653 9827
2609	PC		Castlebay, Barra, Catholic Chapel, &c	-	NL 6659 9827
2610	PC		Catholic Church &c, Castlebay, Barra	-	NL 6659 9827
2611	Print		Man with pack pony in front of St Mary's Church, Castlebay	-	NL 6663 9827
2611	PC		Each Chleibh [Enlargement]	-	NL 6663 9827
2612	PC		In Castlebay, Barra	-	NL 6662 9827
2613	Print	C1738	At Castlebay, Barra [Fishermen's houses and boats]	1897-07-??	NL 6663 9820
2614	Print	C1677	At Castlebay, Barra [A group of men]	1897-07-??	NL 6661 9822
2615	Print	C1683	Hip-ended blackhouse, Kisimul Castle, Barra in background	-	NL 6691 9807
2615A	Print	C1709	Gearrygall, Castlebay, Barra	1901-11-05	NL 6691 9807
2616	Print	C1735	Women gutting herring, Castlebay, Barra	-	NL 6680 9793
2616	PC		Guiteag sgatan aig Bagh-a-Chaisteal, Barraigh	-	NL 6680 9793
2616A	PC		Guiteag sgatan	-	NL 6680 9793
2617	PC		Curing the finest Herring in the World at Castle Bay, Barra, Outer Hebrides	-	NL 6674 9790
2618	Print	C1730	At Castlebay, Barra [Man with pack-ponies]	1897-07-??	-
2618	PC		Pack-Ponies, in Outer Hebrides	-	-
2618A	PC		Pack-Ponies, in Outer Hebrides [Enlargement]	-	-
2619	PC		An am Bagh-a-Chaistel	-	-
2620	PC		A messenger in Barra	-	-
2621	PC		A Creel Pony, Castlebay, Barra	-	NL 6663 9829
2622	PC	OE-211	Fishermen's Huts, Castlebay, Barra [Scottish Home Industries – Manchester Exhibition]	-	NL 6670 9818

Ref No	Type	SLA/NMS Cat No	Title or Description	Date	Island
1901	Print	C244	Two hunters with a brace of swans	-	Harris
2902	PC		'Only a drachm !'	-	Harris ?
2903	PC		Some Highlanders in Uist	-	North Uist
1904	Print	C1737	Woman milking Highland cow	-	North Uist
1905	Print	53-13-36	Crofter's house, North Uist	1896 - ?? - ??	North Uist
1906	Print		A Uist crofter family and their home	-	Uist ?
2907	PC		Picturesque Uist, a New Crofter's Homestead	-	North Uist
1908	Print	C242A	Sheep-clipping	-	North Uist
2908	PC		Sheep Clipping in Outer Hebrides	-	North Uist
1909	Print	C239A	Man and woman building a haystack	-	Uist ?
1910	Print	C1698	Pair of horses pulling pair of harrows [probably North Uist]	1897-05-10	North Uist
1911	Print		Three men in sailing boat at shore, side of hill in background [image reversed?]	-	North Uist
1912	Print	C1716	Donald MacLean's shop ?	1897-04-??	North Uist
1913	Print	C1718	Picnic group	-	North Uist
1914	Print	C3559A	Boys Fishing, Uist	-	North Uist ?
2914	PC		Iasgairachd	-	North Uist ?
3914	PC		Boys Fishing, Uist [Scottish Home Industries – Manchester Exhibition]	-	North Uist ?
2915	PC		Fesgaire [Evening]	-	North Uist
2916	PC		The Stag at Eve in the Outer Hebrides	-	North Uist
2917	PC		Water-lillies in Uist	-	Uist ?
1918	Print	C1727	Blackhouse built on rocky outcrop, prob. Harris [wall at right out of focus]	-	Harris
1919	Print		Blackhouse on rocky hillside, probably Harris	-	Harris
1920	Print	C1696	Blackhouses, woman and pony with peat creel in front	-	Uist ?
1921	Print	53-13-34	Blackhouses seen across water	-	Uist ?
1922	Print	C1681	View across low-lying land and lochs – blackhouses in middle distance	-	Uist ?
1923	Print	53-13-54	House seen across water from boat	-	Uist ?
1924	Print	C1689	House with peat stack outside	-	Uist ?
1925	Print	C1725	Blackhouses with family at doorway	1903-08-12	Uist ?
1926	Print	C1705	Woman, boy and sheep in front of a doorway	-	Uist ?
1927	Print	C1701	Stallion in front of house	-	Uist ?

1928	Print	C1726	Elderly man being helped aboard horse and cart	-	Uist ?
1929	Print	C3560	Man – said to be 103	1896-??-??	Uist ?
1930	Print		Eviction [Two women, one seated, one lying down]	-	North Uist
1931	Print		Eviction [Family group seated among furniture]	-	North Uist
1932	Print		Eviction [Furniture and belongings in front of house – 2 bailiffs]	-	North Uist
1933	Print		Eviction [Two figures at blackhouse door, others against wall]	-	North Uist
1934	Print		Eviction [Two figures at blackhouse door, bailiff in centre]	-	North Uist
1935	Print		Eviction [Figures agaist blackhouse walls]	-	North Uist
1936	Print		Eviction [Group outside blackhouse, bailiffs at table in centre]	-	North Uist
1937	Print		Eviction [Blackhouse with possessions outside ?, hills in background]	-	North Uist
1938	Print	C1736	Stromeferry [Inverness railway terminus]	1892-??-??	Mainland

Fig. A.1: Photographic locations in North Harris shown on Ordnance Survey One-Inch Second Edition, Sheet 98 1896; reproduced by permission of the NLS.

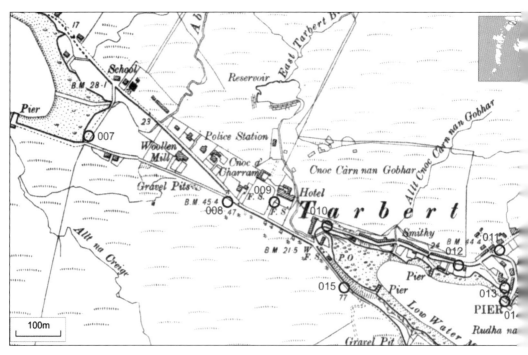

Fig. A.2: Photographic locations in Tarbert area, Harris shown on Ordnance Survey Six-Inch Second Edition, Inverness-shire Hebrides, Sheets XIII and XIV/XV, 1903; reproduced by permission of the NLS.

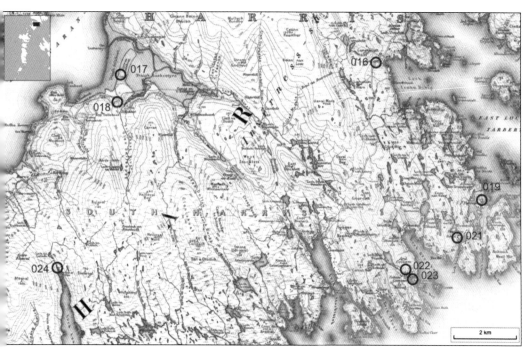

Fig. A.3: Photographic locations in northern part of South Harris shown on Ordnance Survey One-Inch Second Edition, Sheets 89, 90, 98 and 99, 1896–1897; reproduced by permission of the NLS.

Fig. A.4: Photographic locations in southern part of South Harris shown on Ordnance Survey One-Inch Second Edition, Sheet 89, 1896; reproduced by permission of the NLS.

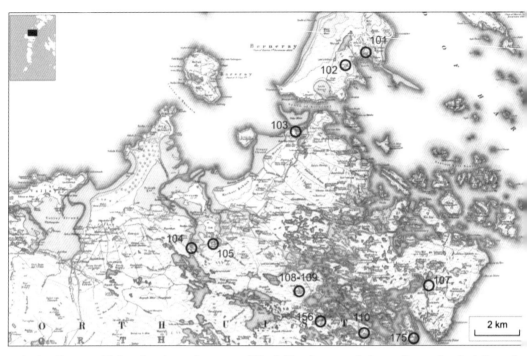

Fig. A.5: Photographic locations in northern part of North Uist shown on Ordnance Survey One-Inch Second Edition, Sheet 89, 1896; reproduced by permission of the NLS.

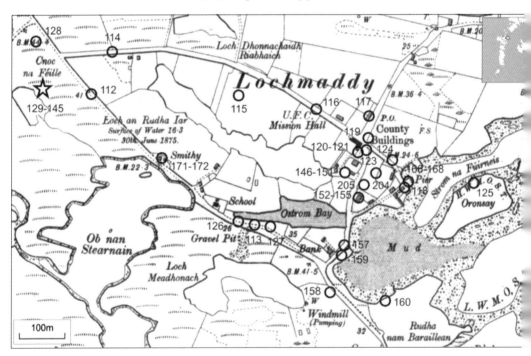

Fig. A.6: Photographic locations in Lochmaddy village area, North Uist Harris shown on Ordnance Survey Six-Inch Second Edition, Inverness-shire Hebrides, Sheet XXXV, 1903; reproduced by permission of the NLS; stars represent generalised locations.

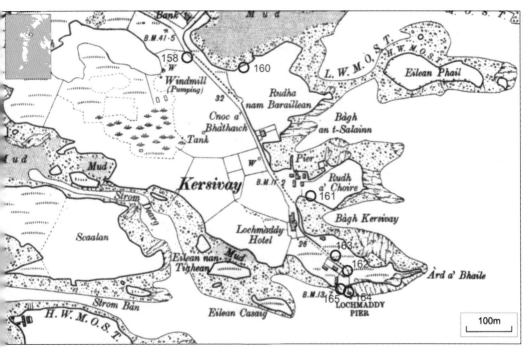

Fig. A.7: Photographic locations in Lochmaddy harbour area, North Uist shown on Ordnance Survey Six-Inch Second Edition, Inverness-shire Hebrides, Sheet XXXV, 1903; reproduced by permission of the NLS.

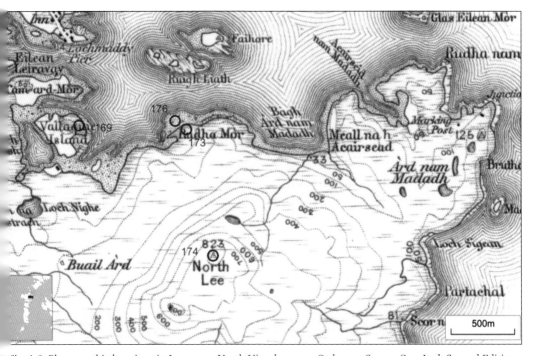

Fig. A.8: Photographic locations in Lees area, North Uist shown on Ordnance Survey One-Inch Second Edition, Sheet 89, 1896; reproduced by permission of the NLS.

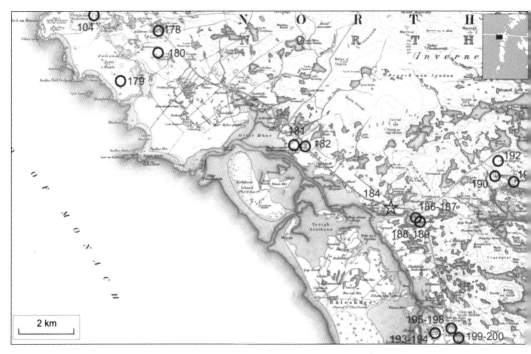

Fig. A.9: Photographic locations in southern part of North Uist shown on Ordnance Survey One-Inch Second Edition, Sheets 78, 79, 88 and 99, 1896; reproduced by permission of the NLS; stars represent generalised locations.

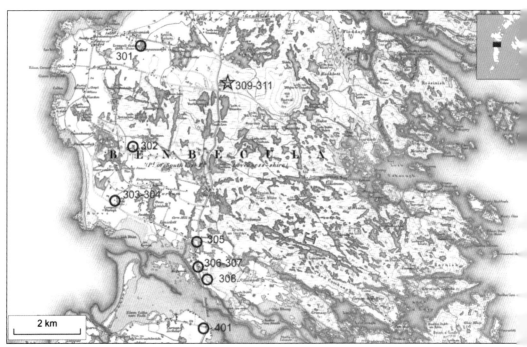

Fig. A.10: Photographic locations in Benbecula and northern part of South Uist shown on Ordnance Survey One-Inch Second Edition, Sheet 79, 1896; reproduced by permission of the NLS; stars represent generalised locations.

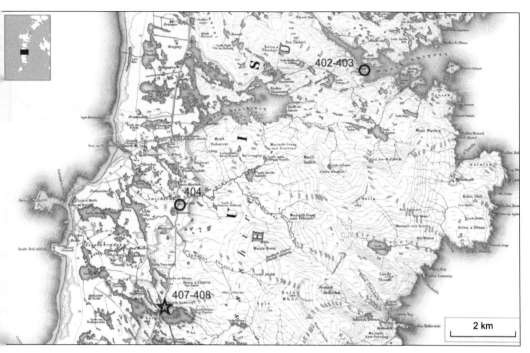

Fig. A.11: Photographic locations in northern part of South Uist shown on Ordnance Survey One-Inch Second Edition, Sheets 69 and 79, 1896; reproduced by permission of the NLS; stars represent generalised locations.

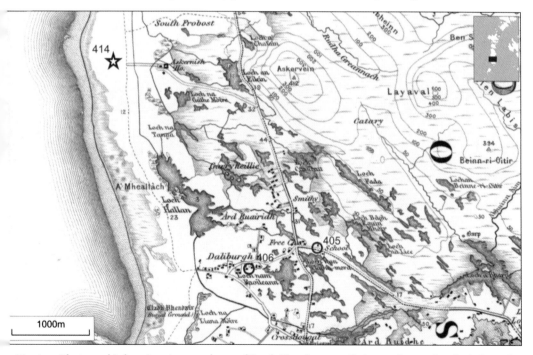

Fig. A.12: Photographic locations in central part of South Uist shown on Ordnance Survey One-Inch Second Edition, Sheet 69, 1896; reproduced by permission of the NLS; stars represent generalised locations.

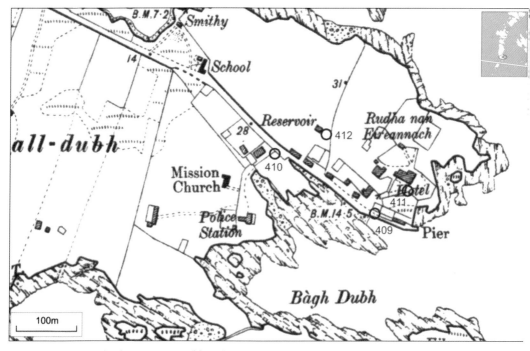

Fig. A.13: Photographic locations in Lochboisdale area, South Uist shown on Ordnance Survey Six-Inch Second Edition, Inverness-shire Hebrides, Sheet LVII, 1904; reproduced by permission of the NLS.

Fig. A.14: Photographic locations in Eriskay shown on Ordnance Survey One-Inch Second Edition, Sheets 59 and 69, 1896; reproduced by permission of the NLS.

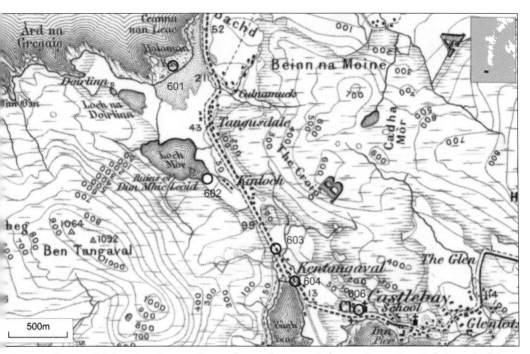

Fig. A.15: Photographic locations in central part of Barra shown on Ordnance Survey One-Inch Second Edition, Sheet 58, 1896; reproduced by permission of the NLS.

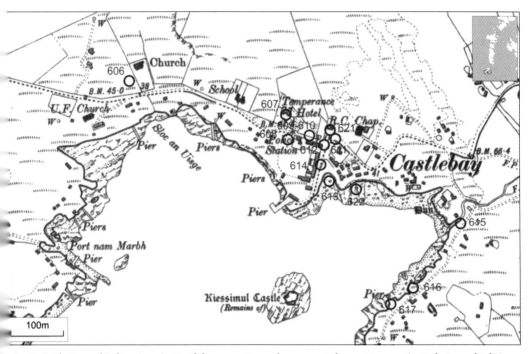

Fig. A.16: Photographic locations in Castlebay area, Barra shown on Ordnance Survey Six-Inch Second Edition, Inverness-shire Hebrides, Sheet LXIV, 1904; reproduced by permission of the NLS.

Appendix 2

Glossary of Place Names in English and Gaelic

Gaelic translations and English alternatives for all place names used in the text are provided in the following glossary. The definitive spellings of Gaelic place names are taken from the latest editions of 1:25,000 Ordnance Survey Maps.

English	Gaelic
Ardhasaig	Àird Asaig
Bala	Am Baile
Balranald	Baile Raghnill
	Balaranuill*
Barra	Barraigh
Benbecula	Beinn na Faoghla
Berneray	Beàrnaraigh
Blashaval	Blathaisbhal
Borve	Na Buirgh
Bunavoneader	Bun Abhainn Eadarra
	Bunamhuinneddor*
Carinish	Cairinis
Carnan	Càrnan
Castlebay	Bàgh a' Chaisteal
Claddach Illeray	Cladach Iolaraigh
Claddach Kyles	Cladach a' Chaolais
Claddach-Kirkibost	Cladach Chirceboist
Creagorry	Creag Goraidh
Crogary Mor	Crògearraidh Mòr
Daliburgh	Dalabrog
Eriskay	Eirisgaigh
Finsbay	Fionnsabhagh
Gearrygall	Gearraidh Gadhal
Gramisdale	Gramasdal
Grosebay	Greosabhagh

Hougarry	Hogha Gearraidh
Howmore	Tobha Mòr
Hushinish	Hùisinis
Kentangval	Ceann Tangabhal
Kisimul Castle	Caisteal Chiosmuil
Langash	Langais
	Langass*
Lochboisdale	Loch Baghasdail
Locheport	Loch Euphort
Lochmaddy	Loch nam Madadh
	Loch-an-madaidh*
	Loch-na-madaidh*
Lochportan	Loch Portain
Loch Skipport	Loch Sgioport
Luskentyre	Losgaintir
North Ford	An Fhadhail a Tuath
North Harris	Ceann a Tuath na Hearadh
North Uist	Uibhist a Tuath
Obbe (Leverburgh)	An t-Ob
Ormiclate	Ormacleit
Rishgarry	Ruisigearraidh
Rodel	Roghadal
Ru Vollarip	Rudha Bhalairop
Scadabay	Scadabhagh
Shelibost	Seilebost
South Ford	An Fhadhail a Deas
South Harris	Ceann a Deas na Hearadh
South Uist	Uibhist a Deas
Stockinish	Stocinis
Strombane	Srom Bàn
Strond	Srannda
Strumore	Sruth Mòr
Tarbert	An Tairbeart

* Alternative spellings used on published picture postcards (see note in Appendix 1).